*This book
was presented to:*

_____

From:

_____

On this day:

_____

Published by B&H Publishing Group
Nashville, Tennessee

1 2 3 4 5 6 • 23 22 21 20 19

CONCRETE & CRANES DEVOTIONS

DEVOTIONS

100 DEVOTIONS

Building on the Love of JESUS

Text written
by Rhonda
VanCleave

B&H kids

Nashville TN

INTRODUCTION

Watching construction crews can be fascinating and amazing, but do you know what I've noticed? Buildings take time! Construction of a building can take weeks or even months. The bigger the building, the longer it takes.

First Corinthians 3:9 describes us as God's building. We are a work in progress, and God is the builder. He uses the people you know and the experiences you have to construct the person you are becoming. God promises that "He who started a good work" in each of you "will carry it on to completion" (Philippians 1:6).

Buildings need a strong foundation. In fact, the taller the building, the deeper the foundation needs to be. Jesus is our foundation. Reading our Bibles and thinking about the truth show us how we build on that foundation.

When I think about the kids in my life, both in my family and at my church, I pray that each of them will discover the strong foundation of love that Jesus is. If I could share a hundred Bible verses that are building blocks of truth, these are those verses. These devotions are constructed in sections to help you as you build.

Devotions 1–18: These devotions focus on God's blueprint for salvation. Our foundation rests on the sure relationship we can have through our Savior Jesus Christ.

Devotions 19–41: How do we know our foundation is sure? The Bible is filled with promises that help us know we believe God's truth.

Devotions 42–98: Once a foundation is set, the building begins to take shape. Some refer to this as "framing." The framework of the building determines what the building will look like. Our framework comes from prayer, Bible reading, study, worship, and fellowship with other believers, and obedience to God. You can find devotions on these topics in the following sections:

Devotions 42–56: Prayer

Devotions 57–70: Bible Reading and Study

Devotions 71–84: Worship and Fellowship

Devotions 85–98: Obeying God

Devotions 99–100: The last two devotions help you think about all you've learned.

I am praying that you will develop a love for reading God's Word and discover how God's truth can build you into the very special person God has planned for you to be.

1

FINISHING THE JOB

I am sure of this, that he who started a good work in you will carry it on to completion until the day of Christ Jesus.—Philippians 1:6

Have you ever started something and not finished? Why? Was it too hard? Too boring? Or did you get interrupted? Most of us have started something but left it forgotten and incomplete. The Bible tells us God has started a good work in each of us, and He will complete it! He never gets bored with us, and He is never interrupted by something else. He is God! He can be involved in the tiniest detail of our lives and the biggest thing happening on the planet at the same time. God promises to help us grow and become exactly the unique creation we were meant to be until the day of Christ Jesus (that means when Jesus returns). Trusting Jesus as Savior and Lord is the most important part of the work God does in us. The devotions in this book will help you understand more about what it means to become a Christian and to follow Jesus.

NAIL IT DOWN

Write the words of Philippians 1:6 (two words at a time) on separate sticky notes until you have the whole verse and reference. Stick those notes to a mirror or wall in your room. Each day, remove a sticky note and see if you can say the entire verse. Keep going until you can say the whole verse from memory.

PRAY

Thank God for making you and for the special plans He has for you.

2

OUNDATION OF SALVATION

No one has greater love than this: to lay down his life for his friends.—John 15:13

Have you ever watched the construction of a building? Did it seem to take forever to get started? Huge earth-moving machines dug deep and pushed dirt around for days. Holes were dug and concrete was poured. Then, they waited. Then, they dug more holes and poured more concrete and did more waiting. That's because a good, strong foundation takes time. You can't skip that step. The rest of the building depends on a good foundation. Our spiritual life is the same way. It begins when we trust Jesus as Savior. Let's spend the next few days looking carefully at God's blueprint for salvation, upon which we build our lives. We must never forget that Jesus provided salvation because of His great love for us. The more we get to know Jesus, the more we'll understand how His love is our strong foundation.

PERSONAL BLUEPRINT

If you've already trusted Jesus as Savior, write about it here. If you haven't, write down some questions or thoughts you still have.

PRAY

Don't expect to know everything about God or the Bible. Adults still learn new things as they read God's Word. Pray and ask God to help you understand what you need to know as you read your Bible.

3

GOD RULES

In the beginning God created the heavens and the earth.—Genesis 1:1

Most everything we know is made from something else. Cookies were once flour, sugar, eggs, and other ingredients that someone mixed and baked. Video games were once pieces of metal and plastic that had to be pieced together. Even your clothes were once strings of fiber or bolts of cloth. We can be creative with what we have and make things we enjoy. But only God can simply speak and create things from nothing. The Bible tells us God created everything, including you and me. Because God created everything, He is in charge of everything. He is all-powerful. When we think about God and His mighty power, we honor Him, and that is worship. God is pleased when we worship Him.

PERSONAL BLUEPRINT

What are some of your favorite things in God's creation? Maybe you saw a beautiful sunset or an amazing bug or the wind making the leaves on the trees dance. Jot down a few of the things you noticed or sketch some of your favorites.

PRAY

Tell God why you think His creation is amazing. Thank Him for some of your favorite parts of creation.

4

GOD IS IN CONTROL

Our Lord and God, you are worthy to receive glory and honor and power, because you have created all things, and by your will they exist and were created.—Revelation 4:11

In the previous devotion you read a verse from Genesis. Today you read one from Revelation. Wow! That's from the beginning to the end of the Bible. The Bible tells us that God created everything and that He is in charge of everything. That's called "sovereign," and it means "totally in control." We know that bad things happen, and as we read more of God's Word in the devotions to follow, we will learn why. However, today let's just think about how truly wonderful God is and how He could create anything He wanted to create. And guess what? He created you! Today's verse tells us that it is because of God's will that we even exist! The Bible also tells us that people are His most special creation—made in His image. You are God's creation.

NAIL IT DOWN

Read Revelation 4:11 again. How do we give God glory and honor? Write some of your thoughts here.

PRAY

Did you know you can make Bible verses part of your prayer? Pray today's verse (Revelation 4:11) to God and think about what you are saying.

5

WE SINNED

For all have sinned and fall short of the glory of God.—Romans 3:23

What do you think is worse—telling a lie or stealing something? What about being rude to another person or breaking something in a fit of anger? Did you know that the Bible tells us all of these are sins? People often talk about "big" sins or "little" sins, but the truth is, sin is anything that goes against what God tell us in His Word. And, Romans 3:23 tells us that we are all sinners. The verse explains that, not only are we all equally sinners, but we all "fall short of the glory of God." That means, no matter how hard we try, we cannot be as good as God on our own. That's where the best news of all comes in. God knows we can't do it on our own. That's why God provided His Son Jesus to do what we can't! As you read the next few devotions you'll discover more Bible verses that help you know God's exciting plan.

NAIL IT DOWN

Can you find Romans 3:23 in your Bible? Write it down here. This is a great verse to highlight and memorize!

PRAY

Praying to God is just talking to God. You don't have to use fancy or special words. He made you, and He loves for you to talk to Him, even when you are admitting to God that you did something wrong. He promises to love you and forgive you.

6

PAYMENT DUE

For the wages of sin is death, but the gift
of God is eternal life in Christ Jesus our Lord.
—Romans 6:23

Do you get paid for doing chores? I've had many jobs, and it's always exciting to get paid. Another word for "payment" is "wages." The word *wages* basically means "getting what you earn or deserve." Romans 6:23 talks about the wages of sin. You've already learned that sin is when we choose to disobey God. Sin separates us from God and sin deserves God's punishment. The rest of the verse, however, has a great promise! It talks about God's gift. Gifts are different from wages. Gifts are given freely no matter what you have done. You don't earn or even deserve them. God offers us the gift of forgiveness and eternal life through Jesus. The next two devotions will tell you more about how God provided this amazing gift.

NAIL IT DOWN

Think about these words and their meanings based on what you've learned so far:

Sovereign—totally in control (God is totally in control)

Sin—choosing to disobey God

Are there other words you are unsure about? Write them here and add the definition when you learn it.

PRAY

People like to hear "thank you" or get a thank-you note when they give a nice gift. God has given the greatest gift of all, His Son, Jesus. Pray and thank God for Jesus.

7

GOD PROVIDED

For God loved the world in this way: He gave his one and only Son, so that everyone who believes in him will not perish but have eternal life.
—John 3:16

John 3:16 is often one of the first verses many people memorize. It may sound slightly different because of the translation each person uses, but the meaning is exactly the same. God sent Jesus, the perfect solution to our sin problem, to rescue us from the punishment we deserve. It's something we as sinners could never earn on our own. Why was Jesus the perfect solution? It is because He came to earth in human form. He experienced everything humans experience, and yet, He never sinned. He was always obedient to God. Because of the things Jesus did for us, He can offer us His free gift of forgiveness. Accepting Jesus as Savior means receiving His free gift of salvation and the promise of life with Him now and forever.

PERSONAL BLUEPRINT

Memorize John 3:16. Writing a verse down is a great way to memorize (or review) a Bible verse. Print the words to John 3:16 in three different locations such as on this page, on a sticky note to attach to your mirror, on an index card to tuck in your Bible, or start a notebook with a collection of your favorite Bible verses.

PRAY

John 3:16 begins by telling us how much God loves us. Talk to God about how you feel about Him.

8

GOD'S GIFT

For you are saved by grace through faith, and this is not from yourselves; it is God's gift—not from works, so that no one can boast.
—Ephesians 2:8–9

Are there chores you have to do that you really dread? For instance, I hate cleaning the cat's litter box. How do you feel when you discover someone else has already done that chore for you? I feel a huge relief! Now, think about something that would be impossible to do, and yet, God has done it already! We've talked about how all of us sin and none of us is able to pay the penalty for those sins. So, God provided a way for our sins to be forgiven through His Son Jesus. Being saved (becoming a Christian) happens because of what Jesus did for us. No one can brag about how good they are or how many great things they have done. Jesus alone saves us when we ask Him to forgive our sins and trust Him as our Savior.

NAIL IT DOWN

Think about the meaning of these words:

Grace—Undeserved love given to people by God

Faith—Belief that what God has told a person about Himself and people in the Bible is true

Saved—Having become a Christian; having trusted in Jesus as Savior and Lord

PRAY

Are you beginning to understand more about who Jesus is and why He came? Ask God to help you understand His Word and learn more about who Jesus is.

9

JESUS GIVES

But God proves his own love for us in that while we were still sinners, Christ died for us.
—Romans 5:8

What have you learned so far? God created everything and is in charge of everything. Even though people are God's most special creation, we choose to disobey Him, which is sin. There is nothing we can do to make up for disobeying God. It took someone who was willing to live a perfect life and take the punishment for our sin. That person was Jesus. Jesus came and died on the cross for our sins before we were even born. Jesus died for us knowing that some would receive His free gift of forgiveness and others would refuse it. But He did it anyway because of His great love for us. Jesus' actions prove His love for us.

PERSONAL BLUEPRINT

Do you know what it means to ponder? It means to "think about" or "reflect on" something. Pondering is good when you are thinking about what you learn in the Bible. For instance, think about how Jesus knew about you and everything you'd ever do even when He was on the cross. But most of all, He loved you, and He proved it.

PRAY

Tell God how you feel when you think about how much Jesus loves you and how He proved it.

10

JESUS LIVES

For Christ also suffered for sins once for all, the righteous for the unrighteous, that he might bring you to God. He was put to death in the flesh but made alive by the Spirit.—1 Peter 3:18

For the last few devotions, we've talked about things that can make us sad, things like sin and death. The truth is that they should make you feel that way because those things mean separation from God, but now we have reason to celebrate and rejoice! Do you see the end of 1 Peter 3:18? Jesus is alive! Yes, Jesus lived a perfect life and took our punishment on the cross, but He has power over sin and death! He arose from the dead and is alive! Because of what Jesus did for us, we can be welcomed into God's family for eternity. This is the best gift ever! The next few devotions will look at Bible verses that help you know how you can respond to this good news about Jesus. Keep reading!

NAIL IT DOWN

Have you ever heard the word *gospel*? It means "good news." It is the message about Jesus Christ, the kingdom of God, and salvation. What good news have you learned about Jesus? Write some of your thoughts here:

PRAY

Thank God for the good news about Jesus, His love for you, and salvation.

11

WE RESPOND

But to all who did receive him (Jesus), he gave them the right to be children of God, to those who believe in his name.—John 1:12

What does "receiving Jesus" or even "believing in His name" mean? As you read the Bible and learn more about Jesus, you begin to understand more about your own sin and why Jesus came and died for those sins. God's Spirit helps you know that you need forgiveness and gives you the desire to trust in Jesus as Savior. You may have heard about "The ABCs of Becoming a Christian." The letters stand for "Admit," "Believe," and "Confess." It's a simple tool that can help you remember how to respond when God's Spirit prompts you to receive the gift Jesus offers. It is also a great tool to tell someone else how they too can receive God's gift of forgiveness. The next few devotions will look at some Bible verses that explain more about how to respond to Jesus.

NAIL IT DOWN

Why is it important to read so many Bible verses about becoming a Christian? That's because we discover God's truth when we study the whole Bible. Sometimes people can make something sound true by reading one verse or a piece of a verse, but truth is found when you study all of God's Word.

PRAY

Ask God to help you learn something new each time you read the Bible and ponder His truth.

12

A—ADMIT

Therefore repent and turn back, so that your sins may be wiped out.—Acts 3:19

When a person realizes he is a sinner and needs God's forgiveness, how do you help him know what to do? The Bible tells us everything we need to know. Many verses and passages explain that we have to admit or acknowledge our sin. Admitting you have sinned is just part of it. After we admit, the Bible says we are to repent. To repent is to turn away from your sin. Repent doesn't just mean turning from doing bad things to doing good things. It goes much deeper than that! It means turning from sin and even from your own good works, and turning to Jesus, trusting only in Him to save you. True repentance changes how you think, not just how you act. Acts 3:19 says that when we repent, our sins are wiped out. That's completely forgiven! Admitting to God that you are a sinner means you want to receive His free gift of forgiveness. When you think about it, God already knows about you anyway!

PERSONAL BLUEPRINT

Have you trusted Jesus as your Savior? There aren't any magic words to use. God knows your thoughts, even before you say the words aloud. In your own words, you can tell God you know you have sinned and you want to repent (turn) and follow Him.

PRAY

Thank God for His Word (the Bible) that helps us know how we can trust Jesus as Savior.

13

IF WE ADMIT TO GOD

If we confess our sins, he is faithful and righteous to forgive us our sins and to cleanse us from all unrighteousness.—1 John 1:9

The words *confess* and *admit* can get confusing. Both mean to honestly say what is true. "Admitting to God you are a sinner" and "confessing our sins" has the same meaning. It might seem hard to do, but look at the amazing promise God put right there in 1 John 1:9! God is faithful and righteous (completely right) to forgive us and cleanse us from all unrighteousness (sin). We can't do it, but God can! He promises that He will when we admit we are sinners. Do you realize that "cleanse us from all unrighteousness" means that when God looks at us, it is as if we have never sinned? Wow! Isn't that mind-blowing! God loves us that much!

NAIL IT DOWN

How would you explain the "Admit" part of responding to the gospel? Today's verse, 1 John 1:9, is a great way to explain it. Mark this verse in your Bible. Copy the verse here or in a journal and memorize it.

PRAY

Tell God how it feels when you realize He will forgive *all* your sins when you trust Him.

14

B—BELIEVE

Jesus told him, "I am the way, the truth, and the life. No one comes to the Father except through me."—John 14:6

People often make a list of the good things they have done that they believe proves they deserve to go to heaven, but, Jesus says He is the *only* way. He is the life! We can't be good enough or do enough to earn our way into heaven. Think about it. Would Jesus have died for our sins if there had been any other way? Jesus willingly took our sins and punishment because He is the only way to be made right (righteous) before God the Father. That's actually very good news. Jesus did what we can't do. Believing Jesus is who He says He is, receiving His gift of forgiveness and trusting Him to be our Savior is how an eternal relationship with Jesus Christ begins. Jesus is the way, the truth, and the life. You can believe what He says.

NAIL IT DOWN

John 14:6 is an amazing verse. It clearly explains that Jesus is the only way to be saved. Can you think of hand motions to help you memorize this verse? Share the verse and your hand motions with someone at home.

PRAY

Thank God for providing Jesus to be the way, the truth, and the life. Ask God to help you understand more about what this verse means as you read your Bible and pray every day.

15

REAL BELIEVING

There is salvation in no one else, for there is no other name under heaven given to people by which we must be saved.—Acts 4:12

I've never met George Washington, but I believe he lived because history tells me about him. Who are some other famous people you know, but you've never actually seen or met? Why do you believe they are real? It may be because people you trust have told you about them or you have seen evidence of what they've done. Many people will say they believe Jesus is real, but they don't act like they believe He is who the Bible says He is. Believing in Jesus is more than just saying, "Yes, I believe Jesus is real." It's knowing that Jesus is God's Son and that He took the punishment for our sin when He died on the cross. And then, He proved His power when God raised Him from the dead. Jesus gave His life so we can believe.

PERSONAL BLUEPRINT

What is the difference between believing a fact (Jesus lived on earth) and believing in a Person (Jesus is God's Son who came to be my Savior)? Write your thoughts below.

PRAY

Talk to God about what you know and believe about His Son Jesus. What does today's Bible verse tell you?

C—CONFESS

If you confess with your mouth, "Jesus is Lord," and believe in your heart that God raised him from the dead, you will be saved.—Romans 10:9

How is "confess" different from "admit"? Confessing does mean admitting to something, like admitting you are a sinner. But according to the dictionary, it means even more. *Confess* means "to tell or make known," and it also means, "to declare faith in." Today's verse describes acting on what you have learned about Jesus. It is responding to the gospel of Jesus Christ. Confessing with your mouth means to tell or make known that Jesus is your Lord. That's declaring to the world that you have trusted in Jesus. The part of the verse that describes believing in your heart means that it's more than just saying words. When you mean something with your heart, there will be evidence that you have trusted Jesus as Savior. You want to follow Jesus and honor God.

NAIL IT DOWN

Read Romans 10:9. How would you describe what it says in your own words? Copy the verse here. Then, write in your own words what you think the verse means.

PRAY

Thank God for giving us His Word to help us know how to be saved.

17

EVERYONE WHO CALLS

For everyone who calls on the name of the Lord will be saved.—Romans 10:13

Do you remember what you read in Romans 10:9–10? As you keep reading, you find the most amazing promise in Romans 10:13. It is so exciting! God promises that if you confess with your mouth and believe in your heart, you will be saved. God doesn't make us wonder or guess. He wants us to be sure of His love, of His forgiveness, and of the salvation He promises. When you confess your faith in Jesus, you are telling God and others that Jesus is your Savior. He is your Lord, which means He is in charge of your life. You want to learn what He says in the Bible and start following Him. This is a new life that begins the moment you trust Jesus and continues for all of eternity.

NAIL IT DOWN

If you understand what it means to be saved and become a Christian, talk to God about what you have learned. If you already trust Jesus as your Savior, think about a couple of friends you can share this great news with and print their names here:

PRAY

Thank God for all the verses in the Bible that help us clearly know how to trust Jesus as Savior and Lord.

18

SURE OF SALVATION

Therefore, if anyone is in Christ, he is a new creation; the old has passed away, and see, the new has come!—2 Corinthians 5:17

It's pretty exciting to walk into a just finished building or house for the first time. Freshly painted walls look so clean. New knobs and handles almost sparkle. Things smell brand-new. There is an excitement about everything being new and making move-in plans.

Beginning a new life in Christ feels very similar. Your new life with Jesus begins the moment you trust Jesus as Savior. Second Corinthians 5:17 explains that anyone who is in Christ is a new creation. You are still the same person on the outside, but you are new spiritually. You actually want to read your Bible. You discover how to pray. You enjoy being with others who also love Jesus. Inside, you really sparkle! See, the new has come!

PERSONAL BLUEPRINT

If you could build a house, what would it look like? Draw a picture here and mark the place you'd create for your special Bible study and prayer times.

PRAY

Thank God for Jesus and His amazing love for us.

19

FOUNDATION OF PROMISE

I know whom I have believed and am persuaded that he is able to guard what has been entrusted to me until that day.—2 Timothy 1:12

"Mom! Why can't I have my ticket?" Emma asked for the third time. Emma was excited about today's family adventure, but why wouldn't Mom let her keep the ticket?

"Emma," Mom said, "I'll keep all our tickets safe with me. I will give you your ticket right when you need it." Mom would be sure everyone's tickets made it and were there when it was time. Mom was the one who made sure everyone had what was needed to enjoy a great family adventure day.

The Bible teaches us that God is the one who makes sure all His promises are kept. God wants us to know the joy of following His Son Jesus and to enjoy all the things He promises in His Word. When you read your Bible, you can trust that what God says is true.

NAIL IT DOWN

The next few days you will read some of God's amazing promises found in the Bible. They are printed in this book, but practice looking them up in your Bible. Pick three or four that are your favorite and mark them with sticky notes.

PRAY

Thank God for His promises. Tell God that you know you can trust Him to keep His promises.

PROMISE TO GO WITH US

The LORD is the one who will go before you. He will be with you; he will not leave you or abandon you. Do not be afraid or discouraged. —Deuteronomy 31:8

What are some things that distract you? Maybe you play a game or watch a movie and don't hear your mom calling your name. Do you think adults get distracted too? Of course they do! Sometimes, they are on their phones or computers or talking to a friend and they forget what time it is, or they forget something they need to do. Being distracted can be a real problem! But, the good news is God does not get distracted. He knows everything all the time. God is with you wherever you go. In fact, this verse says He is there before you even get there. He will never leave you or abandon you. What a great promise! God can make these amazing promises because He is God. He is everywhere at the same time. He is all knowing, ever-present, and powerful.

NAIL IT DOWN

Make a list of the places you go on a typical day or week. How does it make you feel to realize God is with you and He is there even before you get there? God is everywhere at the same time!

PRAY

Think through your day today or tomorrow. Talk to God about each place you will be at and thank Him that He promises to be with you wherever you go.

PROMISE OF COURAGE

Haven't I commanded you: be strong and courageous? Do not be afraid or discouraged, for the LORD your God is with you wherever you go.—Joshua 1:9

Sam was excited to start flag football. At one of the first practices the coach showed the players a skill they would need to learn. Sam thought it looked really hard, but the coach began to teach the team about the skill. He showed them exactly how to hold the ball, how to move their arms to catch it just right, and how to get a really good grip on the ball before running. The coach didn't just say, "Catch the ball and don't drop it." He told them how to do it, and then he showed them how.

Today's verse begins with a command to be strong and courageous. But remember, we don't have to be strong and courageous on our own. God helps us! The rest of the promise proves that God helps and shows us how to do the things He wants us to do.

PERSONAL BLUEPRINT

Print today's verse (Joshua 1:9) on a piece of paper. Draw pictures of places you go and things you do around the edges of the paper. Attach it by the door of your room at home. Read it each time you leave and remember that God is with you and will help you to be strong and courageous.

PRAY

Ask God to help you trust that He is with you even when you feel afraid or discouraged.

22

PROMISE OF REFUGE

Protect me, God, for I take refuge in you.
—Psalm 16:1

What is a refuge? It's a place to take shelter or a place that provides protection. The writer of this psalm sounds like he might have been afraid. Do you know who wrote it? King David! Would you think even a king would be afraid? Everyone feels afraid or uncertain. King David experienced many sad, angry, and hurtful times, but he knew he could trust God, even when things didn't seem to be going well. King David knew that God was his refuge or shelter. King David prayed this prayer to God and you can too. You can trust God even when things don't seem to be going well. Sometimes, God takes care of the problem. Sometimes, the problem may not go away, but God will take care of you.

NAIL IT DOWN

Another great verse to read is Psalm 56:3. Both verses were written by King David and show how he trusted God. Print both verses on sticky notes and place them where you will see them every morning when you leave.

PRAY

Psalm 16:1 is a great Bible verse to use as a prayer too. Try saying it aloud and think about what it means. Next time you feel sad, upset, or afraid, try saying this verse aloud (the louder the better).

23

PROMISE OF HOPE

Rest in God alone, my soul, for my hope comes from him.—Psalm 62:5

Do you ever hope for something special on your birthday or at Christmas? What does that mean? It could mean that you know someone who might get it for you. You hope you are right, but you aren't sure. Maybe it will happen. Sometimes, what you hoped for doesn't happen. That can be very disappointing.

The Bible has verses that talk about hope. But with God, hope is very different. One definition of hope is to "expect with confidence." That's God's type of hope. When God says He will do something, you can expect it with confidence. Today's verse talks about being at rest (relaxed) because our hope comes from God. We don't have to wonder if God will keep His promises. He will! It's a sure thing!

NAIL IT DOWN

Fill this section with words you might use to mean, "expecting with confidence." Here are a few to get your started:

Absolutely!
For sure!
Positive!
Believe it!

PRAY

Thank God for the hope He promises in His Word. Thank Him that the Bible tells us His promises so we know our hope is real.

24

PROMISE OF FORGIVENESS

For you, Lord, are kind and ready to forgive, abounding in faithful love to all who call on you.—Psalm 86:5

"Who wants cookies?" Nana called out as she opened her cookie jar. Nana suddenly looked surprised. "My cookie jar is empty!" she exclaimed. Nana saw that Natalie was looking uncomfortable. "Natalie, did you eat all the cookies without permission?"

Natalie nodded her head. "I did." Natalie was so ashamed. She knew no one else would get cookies. "I'm sorry, Nana. You probably don't even love me anymore."

Nana knelt down and pulled Natalie into a big hug, "Of course I still love you. I am very sad that you made a bad choice. But nothing you can do will make me stop loving you."

That's how God loves us. His love is faithful. Nothing we do could ever make God stop loving us, and He promises to forgive us when we are truly sorry.

NAIL IT DOWN

Psalm 86:5 lists three words or phrases that describe God. List those here:

PRAY

Isn't it a relief to know that, even though our sins make God sad, He still loves us? Talk to God about how you feel when you think about how much He loves you.

25

PROMISE OF LOVE

Give thanks to the LORD, for he is good. His faithful love endures forever.—Psalm 136:1

God loves us because He chooses to love us. We don't earn it. It is a gift. Even when we mess up, God still loves us. Psalm 136 repeats the phrase "His faithful love endures forever" twenty-six times. As the Israelites would sing this psalm, they would remember how God had created everything. They would remember times God had protected them and provided for them. Even when they didn't obey God, He was faithful, and His love endured. To endure is to continue or remain firm. God's love never changes and His love lasts forever. The Israelites sang this song and thanked God for His love. When we talk to God about the many ways He has shown His love for us, we are celebrating God the way the Israelites did.

NAIL IT DOWN

Use your Bible to find Psalm 136. Read verses 1–9 and list some of the things the people praised God for. Then, add nine more things you can praise God for.

PRAY

Thank God for the things you listed and end with praising God that "His faithful love endures forever."

PROMISE TO REALLY KNOW US

LORD, you have searched me and known me.
—Psalm 139:1

Alexa looked at the present her aunt Phoebe gave her. Alexa loved horses and was saving up for riding lessons. When Aunt Phoebe gave her a birthday present, Alexa hoped it would be the final amount for riding lessons. Instead, when she opened the box it was filled with ballet shoes and a pink tutu! PINK! Alexa hated pink. Did her aunt Phoebe even know her?

Sometimes, it can feel like those who are supposed to be closest to us don't seem to know us very well. It can feel like they don't listen to us or ignore our wishes. The Bible teaches us that God knows all about us. He even knows when we sit down and when we stand back up! He knows what we are thinking. Most of all He knows our hearts. That means He knows our desires and the attitudes we have about things, both good and bad. He truly knows all about us.

PERSONAL BLUEPRINT

Use this section as a journal to write down some things you wish others knew about you.

PRAY

Read the list you made in "Personal Blueprint" to God. Thank Him that He already knew all that about you and loves you.

PROMISE OF HIS UNDERSTANDING

Trust in the LORD with all your heart, and do not rely on your own understanding.—Proverbs 3:5

Noah had been staring at the same math problem for what felt like hours. Finally, he tossed his pencil on the table and said, "I just don't get it!" Noah's sister heard what he said and came over to the table to see what was wrong. "I don't understand this problem," Noah said.

"I had this last year. I still remember how to do it. Let me help," his sister said. Before long, Noah figured out the problem. All it took was just a little help from someone who understood the problem like his sister did.

God is like that with us. He has all understanding. Not only can God help us, He wants to help us! We don't have to know everything. We can trust in the Lord. He knows way more than we do!

NAIL IT DOWN

Sometimes, God uses people to help you understand things. Sometimes God uses you to help other people. List the names of people God uses to help you.

PRAY

Thank God for the people on your list. Thank Him for giving you and them understanding when you need it.

28

PROMISE OF DIRECTION

In all your ways know him, and he will make your paths straight.—Proverbs 3:6

What does your family use to get directions to a location? Do you ask someone who knows the way? Do you use an app on a phone? Maybe you have another type of GPS device? Some people still use a paper map. Most people want directions that are clear and easy to follow because making a wrong turn can be frustrating. It is really helpful if someone is with you to direct you to a new place. A good navigator can say, "Turn left." or "It's here on the right." They tell you exactly what to do. The Bible tells us, the more we get to know God, the more we will know the path He wants us to take. He will show us the way we should go.

PERSONAL BLUEPRINT

Copy Proverbs 3:5–6 in the space below. Replace some of the words with pictures that help you remember the word, then practice saying this Bible passage.

PRAY

Sometimes, it is hard to know what God wants you to do. Talk to Him about it. Tell God that you will trust Him to guide you because you want to follow His will. God is always listening.

29

PROMISE OF PERFECT PEACE

You will keep the mind that is dependent on you in perfect peace, for it is trusting in you.
—Isaiah 26:3

"I'll fix it!" Have you ever said that? Some people are just naturally "fixers." But when they can't fix something, they get upset or even angry. That's what happens when we try to do things our own way.

Today's verse, Isaiah 26:3, tells us to depend on God. He will help us think of the things we should and know the right things to do. The more we depend on God the less upset or angry we feel. In fact, Isaiah says we will be kept in "perfect peace." That doesn't mean no problems or that the problems go away. It does mean that you can take a deep breath and feel okay because you trust in God. The things around us might not be perfect, but God's peace always is.

NAIL IT DOWN

Make a list of things or times that make you feel like you have to fix something. Then read each item on the list and say, "But!" then read Isaiah 26:3 aloud. Keep practicing the verse. God will help you remember it when you need it.

PRAY

Ask God to help you trust Him even when you can't fix something that's wrong.

30

PROMISE OF HELP

For I am the LORD your God, who holds
your right hand, who says to you,
"Do not fear, I will help you."—Isaiah 41:13

Carly did not like storms. One night, when the storms were really bad, her family huddled with pillows and quilts in their safe place. Suddenly, the power went off. Carly grabbed her dad's hand and held on tightly until Dad could reach for the flashlight and flip it on. Carly felt safe the instant her dad took her hand. Even though it was still dark for a few minutes and she could hear the storm, she knew Dad was there to help and take care of her.

God doesn't physically hold our hand, but the Bible teaches us that He is that close. He is even closer than our parents or anyone else we trust. He is helping us and protecting us in ways we don't even know. Read the last part of that verse aloud, "Do not fear, I will help you."

PERSONAL BLUEPRINT

Draw a picture of somewhere you sometimes feel afraid or alone. Then print at the top of your picture, "God Is with Me."

PRAYER

When you feel fearful, you can turn this verse into a prayer. "I will not fear because You, God, will help me." Thank God today for His promise to always be with you.

31

PROMISE OF NEW MERCIES

Because of the LORD's faithful love we do not perish, for his mercies never end. They are new every morning; great is your faithfulness!
—Lamentations 3:22–23

What is your favorite time of day? Some people love mornings, especially when the sun first comes up. The morning goes from dark to beautiful colors to bright sunshine in a short amount of time. Many love mornings because they enjoy the thrill of a new day with all its possibilities. The reason we can be excited about each day is because of God's promised mercies. God's mercies are the blessings God gives us that we don't deserve. Each day is filled with God's blessings. When we choose to look for those blessings, we might be surprised. Sometimes God's blessings are seeing something He created like an animal or a beautiful flower. Sometimes it might be something someone says to you to encourage you. Sometimes, you might feel peace even when you have to do something difficult. When you begin to watch for God's blessings, you'll be surprised how many you notice.

PERSONAL BLUEPRINT

Draw a picture of a sunrise and think about God's mercies that are new each morning.

PRAY

Leave a sticky note where you will see it first thing in the morning. Remind yourself to pray and thank God for the new day and for the blessings He has planned for you.

32

PROMISE TO BE WITH US

"And remember, I am with you always, to the end of the age."—Matthew 28:20

Sometimes being alone is nice, but sometimes it can be sad or even scary. Jesus promised to always be with us, but sometimes, we can still feel alone. What do you do when you feel lonely and the people you know aren't around? You probably look for things that remind you of them. Maybe it's a note they wrote to you or something they gave you or even food they left for you. You feel a little closer to them just seeing the things that remind you of them. Can you look around and see things that remind you of God? Maybe you can see some of His creation like trees or birds or flowers. Take time to read your Bible, which is God's message to you. God has given us reminders of Himself to help us know He is with us.

NAIL IT DOWN

Look around where you are sitting right now. Can you find ten things that remind you of God? List those things here, then, take time to thank God for the reminders of His presence.

PRAY

It's okay to tell God how you feel and that it's hard to know He is with you. Ask God to comfort you and help you know He is with you.

33

PROMISE FOR ETERNITY

"I give them eternal life, and they will never perish. No one will snatch them out of my hand."
—John 10:28

The Bible is filled with promises about salvation and about what it means to live life as a Christian. John 10:28 is a great verse because it means that, once we trust Jesus as Savior, He is in control and holds on to us. Nothing will cause Him to leave us. We belong to Jesus forever. We are never alone. Just like a building slowly getting taller, the more we learn about Jesus by praying, reading the Bible, and meeting with other Christians, the more we grow as a Christian. The eternal life that Jesus promised doesn't just mean going to heaven when we die. It means that Jesus is with us right now, loving and helping us as we follow Him.

NAIL IT DOWN

Try memorizing John 10:28. Can you think of motions to help you remember each section of the verse? Practice in front of a mirror as you say the words. Remember the "I" in this verse is Jesus. The "them" and "they" are all those who trust in Jesus as Savior. If you have trusted Jesus as your Savior, you can substitute "Jesus" for "I" and your name for "them" or "they" to see how the verse applies to you.

PRAY

Thank Jesus that nothing can take us away from Him. He is in control and He is holding us.

34

PROMISE OF PEACE

"Peace I leave with you. My peace I give to you. I do not give to you as the world gives. Don't let your heart be troubled or fearful."—John 14:27

What is the most peaceful place you can think of? Some people like to be somewhere quiet. Some people enjoy being outside with all the sights, sounds, and smells of nature. Some think about being on the water in a boat. You don't have to be in a special place to experience God's peace. In fact, you can be in the middle of the worst day with all kinds of sounds and activities going on around you, and still feel God's peace. When you feel overwhelmed, take a deep breath and think about God and how much He loves you. Silent prayer is talking to God in your thoughts. As you pray silently, God can help you feel peaceful. God gives us peace when we need it.

PERSONAL BLUEPRINT

Draw a picture of your favorite peaceful place.

PRAY

Ask God to help you learn to turn to Him when things seem crazy. Thank God for His promise of peace. Try praying with just your thoughts (not aloud). God hears our thoughts!

35

PROMISE OF FAITHFULNESS

Let us hold on to the confession of our hope . . .
since he who promised is faithful.—Hebrews 10:23

What do you think it means to be faithful? The dictionary uses definitions like "steadfast," "firm in keeping promises," and "given with strong assurance." The Bible often talks about how God is firm (sure) in keeping promises. When God says He will do something, He will! You can count in it!

What are ways to remember some of God's amazing promises? Do you like collecting things? What about starting a collection of God's promises that you find in the Bible. You can copy the verses onto index cards, in a journal, or create a scrapbook. Decorate the pages with images that make you think of that promise. Plan times to take out your collection and read through the verses. Keep them in a place you can find and enjoy them again and again.

PERSONAL BLUEPRINT

Do you have a favorite Bible verse? Print it here and then draw designs around it or make some of the words into word art by making the letters look 3-D or like bubble letters.

PRAY

Thank God for His faithfulness and for always keeping His promises.

36

PROMISE OF HIS CARE

Casting all your cares on him because he cares about you.—1 Peter 5:7

Rex was convinced no one cared about him. No one seemed to care what he said or did or even felt. One day Rex saw a Bible verse printed on a card. It was 1 Peter 5:7. What did it mean? Someone had put God's name in the verse. "Casting all your cares on God because God cares about you." Rex started to think about that. Did that really mean that God, the God who was bigger than the whole universe, cared about him? Rex wondered if that could be true. Rex wasn't really sure how to pray so he just began to talk aloud to God as if God were in the room. Rex started to feel better and decided to find someone to talk to about what that verse meant.

NAIL IT DOWN

What would you do if Rex were your friend? How can you help friends know that you care, and most of all, that God cares? Write down the initials of some friends you can pray for who need to know God cares about them.

PRAY

Tell God about the things that are worrying you now. Thank Him for His promise to always care for you. Pray for the friends whose initials you wrote down.

37

PROMISES OF ETERNAL LIFE

And this is the promise that he himself made to us: eternal life.—1 John 2:25

John was one of Jesus' twelve chosen disciples. He was also part of a group of three that were closest to Jesus. When John wrote this book of the Bible as a letter, he was reminding people about things they heard Jesus say. John said that Jesus, Himself, promised eternal life to those who trust in Jesus and choose to follow Him. But what does *eternal life* mean? Does it mean never dying? No, our earthly bodies still die. Does it mean we have to wait until heaven to have eternal life? Guess what? That answer is no too. Eternal life means that our life with Jesus begins the instant we trust Him as Savior and continues throughout our lives, then keeps going throughout eternity. Jesus will guide us in this life as we trust Him and follow Him. And He promises we will be with Him forever.

PERSONAL BLUEPRINT

What do you think "eternal life" means? Write your thoughts here, then from time to time, read what you have written and add to it as you understand more.

PRAY

Ask God to help you understand more about Jesus' promise of eternal life.

38

PROMISE OF GREATER POWER

The one who is in you is greater than the one who is in the world.—1 John 4:4

Do you ever feel afraid when you hear people talk about Satan? It is true that evil and sin came into the world because of his tempting, but Jesus has already defeated Satan. Even though bad things still happen in our world, Jesus knows He has already defeated Satan. When you trust in Jesus as your Savior and Lord, God immediately gives you His Spirit to be in you. God's Holy Spirit helps you remember Bible verses you have read. The Spirit helps you understand things you read in the Bible. God's Spirit helps you know what to say when you tell others about Jesus. The Holy Spirit is the One who is in *you*, and He is greater than Satan who is just in the world. God has all power and He is the One who helps you.

NAIL IT DOWN

It can sound confusing when people talk about God the Father, Jesus the Son, and God's Spirit (the Holy Spirit). Sometimes things are just bigger than we can understand because we are not God. God is bigger and more powerful. That's why we have faith. We trust God who loves us even when we don't understand how He does everything He does.

PRAY

Thank God for being so big and so powerful and still loving and caring for you.

39

PROMISE OF ASSURANCE

I have written these things to you who believe in the name of the Son of God so that you may know that you have eternal life.—1 John 5:13

Have you ever asked someone, "Are you sure? Are you really, really sure?" You may have believed what they told you, but you still needed extra assurance. You needed to be really, really sure. God didn't just put one verse in the Bible to help us know that believing in Jesus (the Son of God) was how to have eternal life. He put lots of verses. The verse you read today, 1 John 5:13, is one of those verses. John (one of the original twelve disciples) wrote this book of the Bible so "that you may know." John knew that people like us would need assurance. When you trust in Jesus as Savior, you can trust Him for today, tomorrow, and for all eternity. That's a promise you can trust!

NAIL IT DOWN

What are more of the "these things" John was writing about? Locate 1 John 5:11–13. What did John talk about in these verses?

PRAY

Thank God for the eternal life He promises for those who believe in His Son Jesus.

40

PROMISES ON TOP OF PROMISES

"Do not fear, for I am with you; do not be afraid, for I am your God."—Isaiah 41:10

We've spent several days looking through the Bible at just a few of God's promises to us. We've read about God's promises to love us, help us, direct us, and give us peace. God has given us promises for what we do every day and what we have to look forward to for all eternity. Isaiah 41:10 packs many of those promises into one verse. It's promises on top of promises! How many promises can you count in this one verse?

As you read the Bible you will often see the words "do not fear" or "don't be afraid." Do you realize that God doesn't want us to feel fearful or afraid? God wants us to know that He is with us. He loves us and wants to help us. He holds on to us! We are secure.

NAIL IT DOWN

Memorize Isaiah 41:10. If you like music, try singing the verse to a tune you know or make up one. You could even create a clapping rhythm and say the verse to the rhythm. You can also create motions to your song or rhythm that helps you remember the words to the Bible verse.

PRAY

Thank God for the promises you've read in the Bible. Ask God's Spirit to help you remember those promises just when you need them.

41

AMEN TO PROMISES!

For every one of God's promises is "Yes" in him. Therefore, through him we also say "Amen" to the glory of God.—2 Corinthians 1:20

You have read many promises of the Bible. Therefore, as we end this section of devotions on God's promises, you might still be wondering if you can believe them. Today's verse is for you! This Bible verse means that Jesus is a resounding "*yes!*" to everything God promised. Every one of them! We believe what God said is true and Jesus came to prove it. Because of that (that's what "therefore" means) we can say "*amen!*" We use "amen" in prayers or when we hear God's Word as a way to say, "Yes," "So be it," or "True!" We honor and glorify God when we confidently say "*amen!*" It's true! We believe what God says. Amen to His wonderful promises!

PERSONAL BLUEPRINT

Which promise was your favorite? Copy it here and decorate the border with images the verse makes you think of.

PRAY

Read aloud some of the promises you read about in devotions 20 through 40. As you read the verse, tell God, "Amen!"

42

FRAMING UP

Unless the LORD builds a house, its builders labor over it in vain.—Psalm 127:1

Our salvation is the foundation (or starting point) of living our lives with Jesus. God's Word is filled with promises that help us know that foundation is solid and secure. After a building has a solid foundation, it is time to frame up the walls so it begins to look like a building. Do you remember Philippians 1:6 from the Day 1 devotion? Jesus started a good work in you and He will carry it on to completion. Today's verse reminds us that the only thing that truly lasts is what Jesus builds. Our faith and belief in Jesus grows as we spend time with Jesus through prayer, Bible study, worshipping with other believers, and obeying God. This is the framework that helps us develop and grow as believers. We focus on Jesus, and He builds us up according to His special plan for each of us.

PERSONAL BLUEPRINT

Which one of the actions listed below do you do really well? Put a star by those. Which ones do you need to work on? Put an exclamation mark by those.

- ❑ Prayer
- ❑ Bible reading and study
- ❑ Worship and Christian fellowship
- ❑ Obeying God

PRAY

Thank God for Jesus who helps us grow as Christians.

43

PRAYER

Pray constantly.
—1 Thessalonians 5:17

"Wait just a minute!" Tim exclaimed. "Did you say pray constantly?" Tim's granddad was reading the Bible aloud while Tim put his model together. "I can't pray constantly. How would I listen when other people talk or pay attention in class?"

Tim's granddad smiled and put down his Bible. "A few minutes ago you were working on your model and I was working on Grandma's clock. You knew I was here. Sometimes you'd ask a question and I'd answer. Then, we both go back to working. We didn't talk all the time."

Suddenly Tim got it. "We weren't talking all the time, but you were there and we knew what each other was doing. We were still there with each other even without words."

"Exactly," Granddad said smiling, "God is always with us, and when we think that way, we are still communicating with God even when we aren't using words."

NAIL IT DOWN

The Bible says God knows our thoughts before we say them out loud. Find Psalm 139:4 in your Bible. What does this verse say about God and your thoughts? Write your answer here.

PRAY

Thank God that you don't have to wait for Him to answer like a phone call. Thank Him for listening even before you think a thought.

44

OUR FATHER

"Therefore, you should pray like this: Our Father in heaven, your name be honored as holy."
—Matthew 6:9

Jesus often went alone to pray. Talking to God the Father was really important to Him. Talking to God (prayer) should be really important to us as well. Jesus even showed us how to pray. You may have heard of "The Lord's Prayer" or "The Model Prayer." Jesus taught His followers about prayer. Matthew 6:9–15 is one of the Bible passages that talks about it. Let's look at the first part of the prayer today. Jesus began His prayer by honoring God for who He is. God is holy (set apart, unique) and yet, He is our heavenly Father. Jesus taught us to focus on who God is first when we begin to pray.

When you see people you really care about and they call your name with big smiles on their faces, don't you feel special and loved? That's what we are doing for God when we begin prayers that are just excited to be talking to Him.

NAIL IT DOWN

On another occasion, Jesus had just finished praying and His disciples asked Him to teach them to pray. Jesus used some of the same words to tell them how to pray. You can find it in your Bible in Luke 11:1–4.

PRAY

When you pray today, remember that God is your heavenly Father who loves you. Spend some time just talking to God about the wonderful, loving Father God He is.

45

GOD'S PLANS

"Your kingdom come. Your will be done on earth as it is in heaven."—Matthew 6:10

When we pray to God, we should remember a few important things. We know that God is our heavenly Father. We can also know that His will or His plans for heaven and earth are perfect because God knows everything that will happen.

When you begin something new like the first practice for a new sport or registering at a new school, does it make you nervous? Does it feel like you are about to do something you know nothing about? Does it help to have an adult who knows what to do who will go with you? God knows everything. He knows the future. He knows we have to make it through the "first day" of school or practice before we are comfortable or even enjoy what we do. God is with us. God helps us do the things we need to.

PERSONAL BLUEPRINT

Draw a picture or write about a time you felt nervous or even excited.

PRAY

What did you draw or write about in "Personal Blueprint"? Pray that God would be with you in that situation. Thank Him that you can trust His plans for you.

46

DAILY BREAD

"Give us today our daily bread."
—Matthew 6:11

Are there days when you are hungry all day? You might have even heard your parent say, "Must be a growth spurt!" You need food each day to help you grow and be strong. When Jesus taught His followers to pray, He included asking God for the things we need. We obviously eat more than just bread, but "daily bread" describes the basic needs we have for the day. Jesus used the word *daily* to help His followers know to focus on today. Parents don't usually pack their kids' lunches today for next month or even next week. Parents usually pack just what their kids need for that day. Jesus taught us that God wants to give us today what we need for today. Don't worry about tomorrow or stress about next week. Think about today and trust God to give you what you need.

PERSONAL BLUEPRINT

What are some things you need daily? List them here or create your own icons to represent those needs.

PRAY

It's easy to worry about having something you need tomorrow or next week. Practice thinking about just today and ask God to help you with what you need today.

47

FORGIVING OTHERS

"And forgive us our debts, as we also have forgiven our debtors."—Matthew 6:12

"But Aunt Deb," Amanda grumbled, "Sasha didn't invite me to go to the movies with the rest of the girls. She didn't talk to me all day at school, and she laughed when I dropped my book."

"Amanda," Aunt Deb said gently. "Remember that Jesus taught us to forgive our debtors."

Amanda rolled her eyes. "Sasha doesn't owe me money. She's just been mean and hasn't acted like my friend at all."

"Forgiving our debtors is not about money. It is about forgiving people. We may feel they owe us an apology or an explanation, but Jesus taught us to forgive them whether they ask for it or not. When we forgive others, then we can go to God and ask Him to forgive us. Our relationship with God is the most important relationship of all."

NAIL IT DOWN

Forgiving people can be hard. Even people in the Bible found it hard to do. Look up Matthew 18:21–22 in your Bible. How often did Jesus tell Peter to forgive? Do you think Jesus meant to keep count or to forgive as many times as it takes?

PRAY

Forgiving others can be hard when you are mad. Forgiving helps you be right before God. Ask God to help you forgive others even when it's hard.

48

ESCAPING TEMPTATION

"And do not bring us into temptation, but deliver us from the evil one."—Matthew 6:13

Dakota was surprised when he read Matthew 6:13. Does God bring temptation? And talking about the evil one sounded scary. Dakota decided to ask his Bible study teacher about it.

"Those are good questions," Mr. Bill said. "You are right. God does not tempt people. James 1:13 assures of that. But we live in a world where we are all sinners and sin does exist. The evil one is Satan. He does exist, but remember that God is more powerful and God is in control. We make the choice between obeying God or following the temptations of the evil one. One of my favorite Bible verses is 1 Corinthians 10:13 that promises us that God will provide a way out of temptation if we are willing to take it. Never forget. God is all-powerful and He loves us. He will help us when we trust Him."

NAIL IT DOWN

Look up these extra verses to help you know what today's devotion is about. Put a check in the box when you've read the verse.

- ☐ James 1:13 (God does not tempt anyone.)
- ☐ 1 Corinthians 10:13 (God gives us a way out of temptation.)
- ☐ 1 John 4:4 (Greater is He that is in you than he that is in the world.)

PRAY

Thank God for His power to help you when you are tempted. Ask God to help you know the escape He is giving you to avoid temptation.

49

GOD HEARS YOUR PRAYERS

*The LORD has heard my plea for help;
the LORD accepts my prayer.—Psalm 6:9*

"How do I know God is really listening when I pray? I can't see Him or hear His voice out loud," Bethany asked her mom.

"Tonight was your birthday dinner, right?" Mom asked. Bethany nodded. "You asked for spaghetti weeks ago. You didn't know when I went to the grocery and bought the ingredients. I asked Grandma to make her special garlic bread. I made the sauce this morning while you were at school. So, lots of things were happening that you didn't see or know about."

Bethany nodded. "I get what you mean. God is listening and answering even if I don't know."

"That's right. You asked for spaghetti and you enjoyed it tonight, but you didn't know all the things that were happening in between. You pray to God and you don't always know how He is working, but trust me. He is! Remember to pay attention when He answers prayers and thank Him for His blessings."

PERSONAL BLUEPRINT

Write down some of the things you are praying about and add today's date. Then, when you know God has given an answer, write down what it was and that date. Keep up with what God is doing.

PRAY

We ask God for many things, but sometimes we forget to notice when He answers. Think about prayers God has answered recently and thank Him for hearing your prayers.

50

GOD IS NEAR

The LORD is near the brokenhearted; he saves those crushed in spirit.—Psalm 34:18

Things don't always work out the way we expect. Sometimes the weather changes plans we were excited about. Sometimes families have to move, and kids have to change schools. Sometimes people say hurtful things. Sometimes even sadder times come. The Bible is filled with reminders that God is very near us during times when we feel heartbroken or "crushed in spirit" (too sad to do anything). Sometimes we may feel so sad that we don't even know what words to pray. It's okay. God knows what we are feeling. The words aren't important. It's even okay to just call on God's name and know that He understands. King David had many times when he felt sad or defeated. He wrote many psalms (songs) about it. Many people like to read the psalms when they feel sad (like Psalm 23).

PERSONAL BLUEPRINT

Did you start a list of God's promises yet? You can add Psalm 34:18 to your list. Copy the verse here. Writing Bible verses is a great way to help you remember them when you need to.

PRAY

Thank God for His promise to be near you no matter what you are feeling, even when you are sad, angry, or upset.

51

GOD IS OUR REFUGE

God is our refuge and strength, a helper who is always found in times of trouble.—Psalm 46:1

Jose came home from school and sat down at the table to finish his homework. Mom was cooking dinner, and it smelled so good. "Boy, it's good to be home," Jose told his mom. Jose's mom asked if anything was wrong. "Not really," Jose replied. "Today we just had a bunch of drills at school. Tornado drill. Fire drill. Lock down drill. By the end of the day, I was just ready to get home where it was safe!"

Mom smiled. "Home feels like your refuge." Jose looked confused. "A refuge is a safe place." Mom said. "You feel secure. The Bible tells us that God is our refuge. Even when we can't be home, God is with us wherever we are. He is always there to help us. We can think about God when we feel insecure. He will give us the strength to do what we need to do."

PERSONAL BLUEPRINT

Can you memorize Psalm 46:1? One way to memorize a verse is to write it three times then say it aloud three times. It might help to memorize a phrase a time. When you think you know it, try writing it here from memory.

PRAY

Talk to God about some places or times when you feel insecure or nervous. Ask God to help you know He is your refuge and He will help you.

52

GOD IS OUR PROTECTOR

Indeed, the Protector of Israel does not slumber or sleep. The LORD protects you; the LORD is a shelter right by our side.—Psalm 121:4–5

Brittney was spending the weekend with her cousin. She was having tons of fun during the day, but Brittney couldn't sleep at night. At home, there were night-lights in the hallway and the sound of traffic on nearby roads. At home, she knew the noise of the refrigerator making ice and her dog's funny noises as he slept, but her cousin lived in the country where it was really dark when everyone went to sleep. The noises from the fields outside were strange and their cat liked to jump around on the furniture. Brittney's aunt found her sitting up in bed using a flashlight to read. "Having trouble sleeping?" her aunt asked. Brittney nodded. Her aunt picked up a Bible from the nightstand. "Here, read Psalm 121. It's my favorite Bible chapter. It says that God never sleeps so He is always watching over us. You will be fine. I'll plug in a night light in the hallway and that might help too."

NAIL IT DOWN

Find Psalm 121 in your Bible and read the whole chapter. This chapter reminds us that God is always alert. That means you can pray to Him at any time, even if you wake up in the middle of the night. God is alert and ready to hear your prayer.

PRAY

Is it hard to imagine that God is never tired and He never sleeps? It's true. Talk to God about some times you are glad He is alert and watching over you.

53

GOD ANSWERS

*Call to me and I will answer you and
tell you great and incomprehensible things
you do not know.—Jeremiah 33:3*

Pastor Richard was helping the preteen class during a workday at church. James was on Pastor Richard's team assigned to gather limbs that had blown down during a storm. While they worked, the kids had been asking Pastor Richard lots of questions and he seemed to know a Bible verse that went with every question. "Pastor Richard!" James finally exclaimed, "How do you know so much about the Bible? Did you go to school for years and years?"

Pastor Richard laughed. "I did go to school, but I've read and studied the Bible for a lot longer than that. The more you study the Bible, the more you learn. I still learn new things all the time. God promises us in His Word that when we call to Him (or pray), He will answer us and teach us amazing things. That's why I'm always excited to pray and study the Bible."

NAIL IT DOWN

Jeremiah 33:3 talks about calling to God (praying) and that God would teach us things we need to know. God uses the words from our Bible to teach us those things. The words in the Bible are His words.

PRAY

Ask God to help you understand what you need to as you read God's Word (your Bible). Ask God to help you want to read your Bible more each day.

54

GOD CAN DO ANYTHING

For nothing will be impossible with God.
—Luke 1:37

Jacob could not understand today's math assignment. He tried really hard to solve the problems. He even asked the tutor, but she was so busy with other students that she hadn't really been able to help him. His church had an after-school homework help program, so Jacob asked Mr. Jackson, one of the volunteers, to help him. "Let's begin by praying about this first and ask God to help us figure this out together." Mr. Jackson said.

"Why should I even pray about it?" Jacob sighed. "It's just too hard."

"Nothing is impossible with God," Mr. Jackson reminded him. "Let's pray. We'll ask God to help me explain it so you can understand. And we'll ask God to help you understand. With God's help we can do this!"

NAIL IT DOWN

Jesus also talked about God being able to do the impossible. Read Luke 18:27 and copy it here. Also read what Paul said in Ephesians 3:20. What is God able to do?

PRAY

Is there something you have trouble believing God can do? Tell Him about it, and then trust Him. Even if the outcome is different than what you had hoped, trust that God is still in control.

55

GOD IS MERCIFUL

Therefore, let us approach the throne of grace with boldness, so that we may receive mercy and find grace to help us in time of need.
—Hebrews 4:16

Allie's day had been awful! Everything went wrong. She struck out at her softball game. She forgot about the science project due tomorrow, and she spilled grape soda on her favorite shirt. After dinner, mom suggested she take a few minutes and pray about her day and ask God to help her refocus and work on her assignment.

"I don't feel like praying. I'm angry and tired and upset!" Allie exclaimed. "I'm afraid God wouldn't even listen."

"Listen to this verse I read today," Mom said. She opened her Bible and read Hebrews 4:16. "We can approach God's throne of grace with boldness. That means it's okay to talk to God regardless of how we feel. We pray so we can receive His mercy. Mercy is God's grace that we don't deserve, but He loves us anyway. He can help us in our need and He can even help us with our attitude."

PERSONAL BLUEPRINT

Think about the different feelings you've had in the past twenty-four hours. Draw emojis to show those feelings (maybe sad, angry, happy, jealous, upset, bored, lonely). Write this across the page: "No matter how I feel, I can talk to God."

PRAY

Sometimes you might not feel like praying. It's okay to tell God that as you begin to pray. Ask Him to help you through.

56

TRUSTING GOD'S ANSWERS

This is the confidence we have before him:
If we ask anything according to his will,
he hears us.—1 John 5:14

"Why does God sometimes answer my prayers and sometimes He doesn't?" Sawyer asked his Bible study teacher. Miss Brown looked up from putting supplies back in the cupboard.

"God always answers," Miss Brown said. "It may not be what we want the answer to be. Sometimes God answers no. Sometimes God answers yes. Sometimes God's answer comes later. We have to wait until He knows the time is right. When we are waiting it can feel like He's not answering. Don't your parents sometimes say not right now?" Sawyer nodded. Miss Brown continued, "The important thing is to always ask for God's will to be done. His will is best. The more we learn to trust Him, the more we will understand His answers regardless of if they are yes, no, or not yet."

PERSONAL BLUEPRINT

What are some things you have prayed about recently? Make a list and mark if God's answer was yes, no, or you're still waiting.

PRAY

Thank God that He always answers, even if it means waiting for His answer.

57

BIBLE READING

All Scripture is inspired by God and is profitable for teaching, for rebuking, for correcting for training in righteousness.—2 Timothy 3:16–17

William was reading his Bible, not because he really wanted to, but because Mrs. Brewer had challenged their class to read their Bibles every day for a week. She had given them a list of verses to read. If everyone completed the challenge, there would be a pizza party. William never turned down pizza! As William looked in the front of his Bible to find the page number for 2 Timothy, he started thinking, *Why are the words in this book so special? Are they really any different from any other book?* Finally, William found 2 Timothy 3:16–17, today's assigned verses, and read them. *Wow!* he thought. *Not only is all Scripture from God but it is important to prepare us for good works.* Then William realized something. God had just answered what he was thinking. Maybe he needed to read some more.

PERSONAL BLUEPRINT

The next few devotions are about God's Word (the Bible) and why it is important. Before you begin, list two or three reasons you think God's Word is important.

PRAY

Ask God to help you understand when you read the Bible. Thank Him for giving His Word to help prepare us for every good work.

58

BOOK OF INSTRUCTIONS

This book of instruction must not depart from your mouth; you are to meditate on it day and night so that you may carefully observe everything written in it.—Joshua 1:8

After Moses died, God chose Joshua to lead the Israelites (God's chosen people). Moses had just reminded the people about God's laws. Joshua also reminded them about the things God said. Moses and Joshua knew that once the people were in the promised land, they would get comfortable and focus on things they wanted. It would be easy to slowly forget to focus on God. Does that sound like us? What are things we get involved in or think about that take our focus off God? Joshua told the people to meditate (think about) on God's words day and night. He told them to talk about it often. When you think about something and talk about it, it becomes important to you. God wants His Word to be important to us. That's why we should read our Bibles every day.

PERSONAL BLUEPRINT

What time do you usually get up in the morning or go to bed at night? Think about a typical day. Beside each time, write the main thing you are usually doing. Where would you add Bible reading?

8:00 – 10:00 a.m.

10:00 – Noon

Noon – 2:00 p.m.

2:00 – 4:00 p.m.

4:00 – 6:00 p.m.

6:00 – 8:00 p.m.

PRAY

Ask God to help you know your best time to read the Bible. Thank Him for giving you the instructions you need in His Word.

59

GOD'S WORD IS A TREASURE

I have treasured your word in my heart so that I may not sin against you.—Psalm 119:11

Do you know how to find Psalms in your Bible? Open your Bible as close to the middle as you can. Usually you will be somewhere in Psalms. You might have to practice a few times, but soon you can open to Psalms almost every time. Chapter 119 of Psalms is the longest chapter in the Bible. It has 176 verses! Most of this chapter is about God's Word. The writer of this psalm talks about how important it is to think about God's Word and learn from it. The writer also knew that God's Word would help him know how to live so he did not sin against God. Do you think it is easy or hard to read your Bible? Sometimes it's hard to know where to start. Many people enjoy reading Psalms. You might begin with Psalm 119.

NAIL IT DOWN

Psalm 119 is divided into sections with eight verses in each section. The sections are labeled according to the order of the Hebrew alphabet. Today's verse is from the second section called *Beth*.

Read Psalm 119:9–16 and list some of the things the writer says he will do.

PRAY

You can ask God to help you read His Word. Even if it's just one verse a day, it's good to make a habit of daily Bible reading.

60

GOD'S WORD IS A LIGHT

*Your word is a lamp for my feet
and a light on my path.—Psalm 119:105*

One morning I hiked with a friend to the top of a mountain to see the sunrise. That meant we had to hike in the dark! I'm afraid of a lot of things, especially the things I can't see in the dark. My friend and I had flashlights. I could just see a bit of the path with the beam from my flashlight. It showed me just enough of the path so I knew where to step. It didn't light up the woods around me, but it lit the path I needed to travel. The sunrise was beautiful and the sunlight was bright all the way down, but I learned a lot from the hike up the mountain. Sometimes we have lots of light and can see everything. Sometimes, we only have enough light to know where to step. God's Word is like my flashlight. It shows me the way I need to go to honor God.

PERSONAL BLUEPRINT

Did you read parts of Psalm 119 yesterday? Try reading Psalm 119:97–104 (the section right before today's verse). How did God's Word make this writer feel? How does reading God's Word make you feel?

PRAY

Thank God for His Word that guides us, teaches us, and helps us know more about Him.

61

THE FEAR OF THE LORD

The fear of the LORD is the beginning of knowledge.—Proverbs 1:7

Daniel was confused by what he had just read in his Bible. The verse said "the fear of the Lord." Was he supposed to be afraid of God? Daniel saw his neighbor, Mr. Arnold, working in his flowers. Mr. Arnold was the first one to invite Daniel's family to church. *I'll ask him,* Daniel thought. *He seems to know about God and the Bible.*

Mr. Arnold smiled when Daniel asked his question. "That's great thinking, Daniel. I'm proud of you for reading your Bible. You are right. Sometimes verses have parts that are hard to understand. It is always okay to ask about them. I can help you with this question. This word *fear* does not mean scared. It is a word that means to respect or honor someone. When we fear the Lord it means we know how all-knowing and all-powerful He is. It means we respect what He says and want to follow His instructions."

NAIL IT DOWN

Proverbs is another book of the Bible that is great for Bible study. Locate Proverbs 1 in your Bible. Read verses 1–6, the verses right before today's devotional verse. What did you learn about the writer? Why does it say these words are helpful?

PRAY

Thank God for the things you've learned about Him. Thank Him for wanting you to know even more.

62

WORDS OF WISDOM

For the LORD gives wisdom;
from his mouth come knowledge and
understanding.—Proverbs 2:6

Solomon became king when his father, King David, died. Solomon was just a young man and knew the job would be difficult. God told Solomon to ask for one thing and God would give it to Solomon. Solomon could have asked for wealth or fame or a long life, but instead, he asked God for wisdom so he could rule the people well. Solomon's choice pleased God and God blessed Solomon with amazing wisdom. King Solomon was considered to be one of the wisest men to ever live. Rulers came from other parts of the world just to meet him and talk with him. Solomon knew where his wisdom came from. That's why he wrote in today's verse that wisdom, knowledge, and understanding all come from the Lord. Many of Solomon's wise sayings can be found in the book of Proverbs.

NAIL IT DOWN

Try locating a few of Solomon's wise sayings. Check off each Bible verse as you find it and read it:

- ❏ Proverbs 11:2
- ❏ Proverbs 12:25
- ❏ Proverbs 13:15
- ❏ Proverbs 14:16
- ❏ Proverbs 15:18

PRAY

After you've read the verses in Proverbs, talk to God about the one that might help you the most. Ask God to help you memorize it.

63

PURE TRUTH

Every word of God is pure; he is a shield to those who take refuge in him.—Proverbs 30:5

What do you think "every word of God is pure" means? Anything that is pure means there is nothing else mixed with it. God's Word is absolute truth. It can be trusted.

Have you ever listened as someone told about something that happened, but you knew it was only partly true? Sometimes, people like to twist things to make themselves sound better or someone else sound worse, but their story isn't completely true.

People also choose verses in the Bible and twist them to prove what they want to prove. The Bible says this is wrong. Studying God's Word means more than just reading a verse. It means really thinking about what that verse means. You need to read the verses before and after the verse. It is important to hear the whole message from God.

NAIL IT DOWN

Find Proverbs 30 in your Bible and read verses 5 and 6. You read verse 5 in today's devotional, but notice verse 6. What caution do you find in verse 6?

PRAY

Thank God that His Word is trustworthy and pure. Ask God to help you learn more as you study your Bible.

64

GOD'S WORD WILL LAST FOREVER

"Heaven and earth will pass away, but my words will never pass away."—Luke 21:33

Did you know that when you read your Bible, you are reading something that was written thousands of years ago? It has been translated into your language, but the truth has been there for centuries. You may be holding one book, but it's actually a collection of 66 books. The Old Testament tells about times before Jesus was born. The New Testament tells about the times surrounding Jesus' life and beyond. Even with all those different writers and all those centuries in between books, as you read the Bible you will realize it all connects. The Bible helps us know about God and who He is. It helps us know why God sent His Son Jesus to be our Savior, and it tells us the plans God has for eternity. God's Word will last forever.

NAIL IT DOWN

Consider these amazing facts about our Bible:

The Bible took approximately 1400 years to write.

More than forty people wrote the books in the Bible.

The Bible is still the number one selling book in the world

PRAY

When you think about how long our Bible has been around and how much people still learn from it, are you amazed? Thank God for what you are learning from the Bible.

65

GOD'S SPIRIT HELPS US REMEMBER

The Holy Spirit, whom the Father will send in my name, will teach you all things.—John 14:26

Annie enjoyed reading her Bible. She often copied down Bible verses in her journal so she could remember them, but sometimes, Annie would read her Bible and just feel confused. She decided to ask her Grandpa. He read his Bible a lot. "I learn new things all the time!" Grandpa explained. "I've learned to trust God to help me understand the things I need to understand. Did you know that's one reason God has given us His Holy Spirit? God's Spirit helps us understand things we read in the Bible. That's why sometimes we realize a truth we didn't know before. God's Spirit also helps us remember verses we've learned when we need them."

"Like the verse about not being afraid when I had to give a speech in class last week?" Annie remembered.

"Exactly," said Grandpa. "The Bible is more than a book, and God's Spirit is our Teacher. He helps us know what God wants us to know."

PERSONAL BLUEPRINT

Do you have a journal where you can write down verses you like or that help you? It can be a notebook or notecards. You can also use a highlighter in your Bible or devotional books (like this one) to mark Bible verses you want to remember.

PRAY

Thank God for His Holy Spirit who helps us as we read our Bible and helps us remember the verses we have learned when we need them.

THINKING ABOUT GOD'S WORD

Whatever is true, whatever is honorable, whatever is just, whatever is pure, whatever is lovely, whatever is commendable . . . —Philippians 4:8

Collin flopped over and looked at the clock. He had been in bed for two hours and couldn't go to sleep. His mom heard him and came to see what was wrong. Collin told his mom he couldn't sleep. She asked what he had been doing before he went to bed. Collin admitted he had been playing video games. Instead of being upset, Mom said, "Last night you were reading your Bible before you turned your light out. You went right to sleep."

"I thought just reading words made me sleepy." Collin admitted.

"The Bible tells us that we should put good things in our minds. Often what we have read, seen, or thought about right before bed sticks with us when we try to sleep. We need to dwell or think about good things. Why don't you read Philippians 4:8, then try to go to sleep? I think it will help."

PERSONAL BLUEPRINT

Reading your Bible is one way to dwell on things that are "true, honorable, just, pure, lovely, and commendable." What are other ways you can dwell (or think) on these things? Make a list of things you can think about that would qualify for the list in Philippians 4:8.

PRAY

Praising God for His creation and His blessings are honorable and commendable things. Praise God for these things while you pray.

67

THE WORD OF GOD

For the word of God is living and effective and sharper than any double-edge sword, penetrating as far as the separation of soul and spirit, joints and marrow. —Hebrews 4:12

My favorite book when I was younger was *Little Men*. I wanted to be Miss Jo when I grew up. I read that book until the covers fell off, but do you know what? There were never any surprises or new parts of the story. It was the same story every time with the same ending. Every book I know is like that except for one, the Bible. The more I read my Bible, the more I learn. Sometimes, a verse I memorized will mean even more to me than it did when I first read it. Sometimes I'm even surprised by something I didn't remember reading. God's Holy Spirit is the teacher that helps us learn from God's Word. That's why Hebrews 4:12 says that the Word of God is *living*. The Bible is filled with new things for us to learn about God and His truth.

PERSONAL BLUEPRINT

Do you like to draw? How would you illustrate Hebrews 4:12? Draw your illustration in this space.

PRAY

God's Word is amazing. Thank God for something you have learned recently as you read your Bible.

68

ASK GOD

Now if any of you lacks wisdom, he should ask God—who gives to all generously and ungrudgingly—and it will be given to him.
—James 1:5

Are you sometimes afraid to ask questions? Are you afraid your questions will make you sound less smart than everyone else? The truth is that many people feel that way from time to time. Just remember, no one knows everything—even when they act like they do. God welcomes our questions. As you study your Bible, you will have questions. As you follow Jesus, you will sometimes be unsure about what you should do. James 1:5 contains a great promise for all of us. It says we can ask God for the wisdom we need, and He will give us what we need generously and freely. Another verse in the Bible tells us God knows what we need before we even ask, so God is not surprised by your question. He wants you to ask.

NAIL IT DOWN

Remember to read the verses around a Bible verse to truly understand it. Locate James 1:6 in your Bible. What does this verse say about how we should ask?

PRAY

Thank God for His promise of wisdom. Ask God to help you ask for the wisdom you need in faith without doubting.

69

DOERS OF THE WORD

But be doers of the word and not hearers only, deceiving yourselves.—James 1:22

"Sadie!" Mom exclaimed when she picked her up from play practice. "I know I told you to change your shirt before Mrs. Markum picked you up this afternoon. You have a chocolate stain on the front."

Sadie looked down in dismay. She remembered now that mom had told her to change. She even noticed the chocolate stain herself when she looked in the mirror at home, but she was running late and was packing her backpack when Mrs. Markum came. Sadie had raced out the door, forgetting all about what she had seen and what Mom had told her to do.

The Bible says we do the same thing when we read what the Bible says but then don't do what it says. If we feel proud of ourselves for reading the Bible, but our actions don't match what we read, the Bible says we are deceiving ourselves.

NAIL IT DOWN

Remember to dig deeper and really "nail it down" when you read a Bible verse. Check out James 1:23–25.

PRAY

We all get busy and forget what we know the Bible says to do. Ask God to help you remember His Word as you go about your day.

70

GOD'S FOREVER WORD

But the word of the Lord endures forever.
And this word is the gospel that was
proclaimed to you.—1 Peter 1:25

The last few devotions have focused on reading and studying God's Word. Most of the things we do and enjoy don't last. You may like baking, and people enjoy your cakes or cookies, but after they've been eaten, they're gone. Some things might last for a few years like a painting, a song, or a quilt, but circumstances happen and things can be lost or destroyed. Do you remember how long we said the Bible has been around? Hundreds of years! God says that His Word will endure forever. In our Bible, we read about promises God has already fulfilled and about promises for the future. The Bible is the good news about Jesus and about God's love for us. God's Word will last!

PERSONAL BLUEPRINT

When is your best time to read God's Word? Answer these questions about your personal time with God:

When? (When is the best time for you to have quiet time with God?)

Where? (Where is the best place for you to daily focus on God?)

How? (How do you like to read your Bible and pray? Do you talk out loud or think? Do you write or just read?)

PRAY

Ask God to help you develop the great habit of spending time with Him each day.

71

WORSHIP AND FELLOWSHIP

Not neglecting to gather together, . . . , but encouraging each other.—Hebrews 10:25

Vacation Bible School had been so much fun. Family night was over and only a few people were left at the church. "Can we go home now?" Caroline asked.

"Not yet," Aunt Candace answered. "I have to clean up my room so it's ready for Sunday." A couple of Aunt Candace's friends offered to help. Caroline, her aunt, and the other ladies laughed and talked while they took down decorations and straightened the room. On the way home Caroline said, "That went faster than I thought, and it was kind of fun."

"Christian friends are really important," Aunt Candace explained. "Friends who love Jesus are true blessings. We worship together, spend time together, and encourage each other. That's what is called Christian fellowship. We all love Jesus and help each other."

NAIL IT DOWN

We learn from the Bible about worshipping God. We also learn how Christians work together to help each other and serve God. The next few devotions will look at some of those Bible verses.

Find Hebrews 10:24 in your Bible (the verse before today's verse). What does it say we are to do for one another?

PRAY

Thank God for friends who love Jesus and want to help you. They are true blessings.

72

GENERATION TO GENERATION

*I will sing about the LORD's faithful love forever;
. . . to all generations with my mouth.—Psalm 89:1*

Sara and Hannah stood with their parents for baby Jessie's dedication at church. Hannah held Sara's hand and smiled. Hannah had asked her mom that morning what a baby dedication was. She had been too little to remember Sara's. Mom had explained that it's a special time when parents thank God for their new child. They promise God that they will teach that child about Him. They make the promise in front of their friends at church because it is a serious promise. The people in the church also promise to help teach the child about God. Some of those people will one day teach the child in a Bible class. Everyone promises to pray for the child. Hannah liked that idea. While she stood there, she looked at the faces of people who made that promise when she was a baby. She saw many who were her teachers at church now. They were keeping their promise.

NAIL IT DOWN

Do you know what the word *generations* means? It's a group of people about the same age. You and your friends are a generation. Your parents are part of another generation. Each generation has told the next one about God. That is proclaiming God's faithfulness.

Write your family members' names here:

PRAY

Thank God for family members who may have told you about God. Ask God to help you tell other family members about Him.

73

WORSHIPPING GOD

Come, let us worship and bow down; let us kneel before the LORD our Maker.—Psalm 95:6

Mia's family had moved to a new town. Many things were different from where they used to live. Mia had a new school. She went to a new doctor. The grocery store was different from their old one. They were even looking for a new church to attend in their new town. Each Sunday, they attended a different church. Mia noticed that all the churches did things a little differently. None of them felt exactly like their old church. When Mia asked her dad about it, he said, "People sometimes have different ways of doing the same thing. Churches often have different ways of worshipping, but if it is truly worship, it will accomplish the same thing. It should show honor and respect for God. It should point our thoughts to God. It should also help us focus on what the Bible tells us."

PERSONAL BLUEPRINT

What are some things your church does during worship time? Which parts help you focus the most on God? Write about why that part of the worship time helps you focus on God.

PRAY

Thank God for your church. Ask God to help those who lead in worship to honor Him in all they do.

WORSHIP WITH SONGS

Serve the LORD with gladness; come before him with joyful songs.—Psalm 100:2

Jake loved to sing. He sang in the shower. When he was alone in his room, he sang at the top of his lungs. One day his dad said, "Jake, children's choir is starting at church. Why don't you join? I think you would like it."

Jake's eyes got really big. "Sing where people can hear me? I'd be too embarrassed. What if they think I sound awful?"

"First, you don't sound awful. You sound joyful because you enjoy singing." Dad said. "Singing is one way to serve the Lord especially when you do it with joy. I know Miss Deborah who teaches kids choir. She helps people learn how to use their best voice. You should give it a try. You might like it and you might make friends with other kids who enjoy it too."

NAIL IT DOWN

Music is just one of many ways to worship God. You read one verse from Psalm 100 today, but the whole chapter talks about ways to praise and worship God. Locate Psalm 100 in your Bible. What are some other ways listed in this Psalm?

PRAY

Do you like to sing? Have you ever sung a prayer to God? Sing your favorite song or make up a song, but think about God and sing it as a prayer.

75

WORSHIP ATTITUDE

This is the day the LORD has made;
let us rejoice and be glad in it.—Psalm 118:24

The bunkhouse door flew open, and Evan's camp counselor bounced in, "This is the day the Lord has made!" he shouted at the top of his lungs. "Let us rejoice and be glad in it!"

Evan pulled the covers over his head and groaned. What was good about this day? He had sprained his ankle yesterday, so no sports today. He lost his watch so he had no alarm. And to top it all off, ants had taken over his suitcase. Evan heard his counselor's footsteps stop next to his bunk. "Hey, Evan," he said in a kind voice. "I know yesterday was a rough day for you, but God's mercies are new every morning. We can start each day with an attitude of worship. Here's your suitcase. We got all the ants out and your clothes are fine. After you get dressed, I'll help you get to the mess hall for breakfast. Then, we'll figure out your day from there. You can do this."

NAIL IT DOWN

Some days are hard, but God gives us a fresh start every day. Evan's counselor mentioned verses about God's mercies being new every morning. You can read it in Lamentations 3:22–23.

PRAY

We all have days we wake up in a bad mood, but each day God gives us a new day we can rejoice in. Begin each day by thanking God for that day no matter what.

76

PRAISING GOD

Let everything that breathes praise the LORD. Hallelujah!—Psalm 150:6

Levi was excited about learning to play the trumpet. He had been practicing and thought he sounded pretty good. "Mom," he said one day, "I want to play my trumpet at church next Sunday. I'm getting really good and I want people to hear me."

"Levi," Mom replied. "I'm glad you are excited about playing the trumpet, but do you want to play at church so people will praise you or because you want to use it to praise God? The Bible talks about many instruments that were used in worship to praise God. If it is true worship, people will be thankful to God rather than the performer. If you think about God when you play and do your best for Him, then you are praising God with your talent."

NAIL IT DOWN

Psalm 150 is the last chapter in the book of Psalms. The last five chapters begin and end with the word *hallelujah*, which means "Praise God." Find Psalm 150 and list some of the instruments they used to praise God.

PRAY

You might not play an instrument, but there are other ways to praise God. When you pray, praise Him for helping you know about Him.

77

HONORING GOD

*LORD, you are my God; I will exalt you.
I will praise your name, for you have
accomplished wonders, plans formed long
ago, with perfect faithfulness.—Isaiah 25:1*

Praising God includes remembering the things God has done. We can praise God for big things like creating the world and loving the world so much that He sent Jesus. We can praise God by thanking Him for the wonders we see around us like rainbows and sunsets. We honor God when we remember His faithfulness each day. God provides people who care for us. He provides food for us to eat. He meets our needs. Isaiah said that God has faithfully completed the plans God made long ago. We learn about God as we read in the Bible about the things He has done. Because of what we know about God, we can praise Him and worship Him. He is the One True God.

NAIL IT DOWN

The word *exalt* means to elevate or raise up with praise. When we exalt God, we are honoring Him as the One True God. Can you find these other Bible verses that talk about exalting God?

> Psalm 68:4
>
> Psalm 69:30
>
> Psalm 118:28

PRAY

Praise God for being the Creator. Thank Him for all the specific things He has done for you.

78

WITNESS TO OTHERS

About midnight Paul and Silas were praying and singing hymns to God, and the prisoners were listening to them.—Acts 16:25

Paul and Silas had done nothing wrong. They had been preaching about Jesus, but they had been arrested and thrown in prison. Their feet were chained. They had no idea what might happen the next morning. What do you think you would do if that happened to you? Paul and Silas prayed and sang songs to God. In fact, they were still singing around midnight, and the other prisoners were listening to them. Think about that. They had been treated unfairly. They could have been complaining or even just sleeping. But instead, they chose to take the time to worship God. The other prisoners listened to the songs and prayers. Paul and Silas were being witnesses for God. God protected them in an amazing way and they were able to tell the jailer about Jesus!

NAIL IT DOWN

The whole story of Paul and Silas is very interesting. You can read about it in Acts 16:22–34.

PRAY

Ask God to help you praise Him no matter what your circumstances are. Ask Him to help your praise be a witness to those around you.

79

WORK TOGETHER

*Now as we have many parts in one body,
and all the parts do not have the same
function, in the same way we who are many
are one body in Christ.—Romans 12:4–5*

Blake was helping Pastor Mike put things away after kids' worship one Sunday. "Pastor Mike, I want to be like you someday. It's so fun to listen when you teach. I want to be on the stage and have people listen and get excited when I talk."

"That's really special that you feel that way, but you need to see if that's what God has planned for you. The Bible says that people in the church are like parts of the body. We'd look pretty silly if our bodies were just a bunch of eyeballs or feet." Blake laughed imagining the silly looking body. Pastor Mike continued, "God gifts some people to be teachers, some to serve others, some to encourage, and some to cheerfully show mercy, but when we all do our parts to honor God, then we have a healthy church body that honors God."

PERSONAL BLUEPRINT

God has plans for you as you follow Him. What are some things you enjoy doing? List them here and think how God could use those things to honor Him.

PRAY

Ask God to help you know how you can best serve Him. He is equipping you to do things for Him and when you follow His plan, you will find joy.

80

CARE FOR OTHERS

Love one another deeply as brothers and sisters. Outdo one another in showing honor.
—Romans 12:10

"Why are we going to the store now?" Lainey asked. "I thought we got groceries yesterday."

"They're not for us," Mom replied. "Mr. Owen has been out of work for a long time, and his family has had a lot of medical bills. Our small group at church decided to do a surprise secret blessing for the family. I'm glad. Caring for each other's needs is part of Christian fellowship."

"Their daughter, Kelsey, is in my group at church. I thought she seemed sad, but she didn't say anything." While they were shopping Lainey helped her mom pick out things she thought Kelsey would like. When they finished, Lainey and her mom took the things by the church. They all signed a "Thinking About You" card to let the family know they were prayed for and loved.

PERSONAL BLUEPRINT

Think about people at your church who need to feel that someone cares. Choose one person and write the name here. Write down what you could do to show you care, such as write a card or invite them to sit with you in small group.

PRAY

Ask God to show you someone you can show a special kindness to.

81

COMFORT OTHERS

He comforts us in all our affliction, so that we may be able to comfort those who are in any kind of affliction.—2 Corinthians 1:4

"Mom, remember when I broke my arm last year?" Ella asked.

"I sure do. It was the hand you write with. School work was a real challenge." Mom replied.

"Well, my friend, Olivia came to school today with her arm in a cast. I asked if I could be her helper. I remember things that were hard for me to do, and our teacher said it was okay, so we sat together, and I helped her. I fixed a pillow for her to rest her cast on so her arm doesn't get so tired."

"Ella, I'm really proud of you. You remembered things that comforted you, and now, you can comfort your friend." Mom said as she gave Ella a big hug.

PERSONAL BLUEPRINT

Good things can come from even bad times. You can be a real help to someone who is having a hard time when you've been through the same thing. Think about a time that was hard for you and write about it here.

PRAY

Thank God for helping you during the difficult time. Ask Him to show you when you can share comfort and compassion with someone else.

82

BEING A CHURCH

Speaking to one another in psalms, hymns, and spiritual songs, singing and making music with your heart to the Lord.—Ephesians 5:19

Have you ever thought about why we have church? We need to be together to pray and sing and listen to God's Word. We learn in the Bible that worshipping together is important. When we are with other people who love Jesus, it increases our joy as we worship. "Making music with your heart" means that you worship God with your feelings and attitude. That can be a lot easier when people all around you are doing the same thing. We help each other and pray for each other. We often refer to those we worship with as our "church family." That's because those who are followers of Jesus are brothers and sisters in Christ. God designed us to have fellowship with Him and with each other.

NAIL IT DOWN

Fellowship means close relationship. Fellowship with God means we are getting to know God better. Fellowship with our church family means spending time together, especially when we worship God. What are times you spend with people at your church?

PRAY

Think about your church family and thank God for the people at your church.

83

WORSHIPPING TOGETHER

Let the word of Christ dwell richly among you, . . . through psalms, hymns, and spiritual songs, singing to God with gratitude in your hearts.—Colossians 3:16

"Why do you go to church every Sunday? Is it really that special?" Ayden asked. Brent wasn't sure what to say. His family always went to church on Sunday. He never really thought about why.

Later, Brent told his mom about Ayden's question. "Why do we go to church every Sunday? Is it a rule or something?"

"We honor God by taking time away from our normal schedule and focusing on Him. We gather with other believers because the Bible helps us know that we should. Spending time alone with God is good. Our family tries to do that during the week, but worshipping God with other believers is a time to learn from the Bible together, to sing together, to pray together, and to thank God together. It is special because we are encouraged to follow Jesus when we fellowship with our church family."

PERSONAL BLUEPRINT

Draw a picture of the church you attend. List some things by the picture that your church family does to honor God.

PRAY

Thank God for your church. Thank Him for the place where your church meets. Thank Him for the leaders who preach and teach at your church.

84

REJOICE

Rejoice always.
—1 Thessalonians 5:16

We can talk to God about anything. We can be honest with God about our feelings. So, how do we "rejoice always" like today's Bible verse tells us to do? When King David wrote many of the Psalms, he started out angry, scared, or depressed. He honestly told God how he felt, but King David didn't stop there. After he wrote about himself, he began to write about how good and faithful God is. Before long, King David was singing about joy. Joy can mean happy and laughing, but it can also mean feeling hopeful and glad even when things are looking bad. To rejoice means to have joy or great delight. We are loved by the Creator of the whole universe. He knows everything that is happening everywhere, and yet, He still cares about the smallest detail of your day. That is a reason to feel loved and rejoice.

NAIL IT DOWN

Many psalms begin sad but end joyful. Locate Psalm 5. What words let you know King David was upset at the beginning of the psalm? How do you know King David was rejoicing by the end of the psalm?

PRAY

No matter how you feel, take time to pray to God about His awesome love and power. Begin to name the ways He blesses you. See how your feelings change.

85

OBEYING GOD

As the Father has loved me, I have also loved you. Remain in my love. If you keep my commands you will remain in my love.
—John 15:9–10

Your actions often show how you really feel. If you say you love God but aren't nice to others, your actions don't match your words. Jesus said that if we really love Him, we will keep His commands. Jesus told us to love God with all our heart, soul, mind, and strength. He also said to love our neighbors the way we love ourselves. God's commands focus on loving God and loving others. Sometimes we don't follow those commands the way we should. We disobey what God commanded and that is sin, but God promises to forgive us when we ask. God's forgiveness allows us to continue to remain in the love of Jesus.

NAIL IT DOWN

Three of the gospels record what Jesus said about these two great commandments. Find them in your Bible and put sticky notes next to them.

Matthew 22:37–39

Mark 12:30–31

Luke 10:27

PRAY

Spend some time in prayer today letting God know how much you love Him. Ask God to help you love the people around you.

86

THE MOST IMPORTANT THING

Fear God and keep his commands, because this is for all humanity.—Ecclesiastes 12:13

What is it that every kid you know wants? How did you hear about it? Whether you heard about it from commercials or pop-up ads, what you are experiencing is something every generation experiences. We become convinced that the next best thing is exactly what we need, and we'll be happy. King Solomon was the richest man alive during his time. You may remember reading about him in an earlier devotion. He was very wise. He also became very wealthy and powerful. King Solomon wrote another book of the Bible. It's called Ecclesiastes. After Solomon was older he wrote today's Bible verse. King Solomon was basically saying, regardless of what the world might say you should have, the most important thing is to fear (honor) God and keep His commands.

PERSONAL BLUEPRINT

Draw a picture of something you are really hoping to have soon. It's okay to hope for things you will enjoy as long as honoring God is the most important thing to you.

PRAY

Thank God for the many things you do have. Tell God you want to honor Him with the blessings He gives to you.

87

SO OTHERS WILL KNOW

"I give you a new command: Love one another. Just as I have loved you, you are also to love one another. By this everyone will know that you are my disciples, if you love one another."—John 13:34–35

Micah and his dad were at the hardware store. A lady Micah didn't know suddenly stopped them. "Oh my goodness! It's so good to see you!" The lady exclaimed to Micah's dad. Then, she looked at Micah, "And this has to be your son. He reminds me so much of you at that age."

"This is Mrs. Welch." Micah's dad told him. "She was my teacher in fourth grade. She really helped me with math." As Micah's dad and Mrs. Welch continued to talk, Micah thought about how many people thought he and his dad were alike.

Sometimes, we remind people of our family members, but we can also remind them of Jesus. When we love others the way Jesus did, people begin to recognize that we are followers of Jesus.

NAIL IT DOWN

You can read an interesting verse about two of Jesus' disciples being recognized because they had been around Jesus. You can find the verse in Acts 4:13 or the whole story in Acts 4:5–13.

PRAY

Ask God to help you live each day so others will know that you love Jesus.

88

ACTIONS PROVE IT

"If you love me, you will keep my commands."
—John 14:15

Mom noticed Barlow's empty dog dish when she went to the kitchen to start dinner. "Katy!" Mom called. "Did you feed Barlow today?"

Katy rushed into the kitchen. "I'm sorry, Mom. I was busy, and I just forgot."

"You really wanted a dog, Katy, but lately, you keep forgetting to feed him. Do you still care about Barlow?" Mom asked.

Katy looked surprised. "Of course I do! I love Barlow!"

"When you forget to take care of him, it looks like you don't care about him. Our actions show what is important to us. When you forget to take care of your dog, it seems like he isn't important to you anymore."

"I'm sorry, Mom. Barlow is very important. I'll even put a reminder on my watch so I don't forget."

PERSONAL BLUEPRINT

Jesus said that, if we love Him, we will keep His commandments. Write about things you have done recently that show you love Jesus.

PRAY

It's easy to get distracted and forget to do the things you should. Ask God to help you as you try to obey the things Jesus taught us.

89

TAKING THE RISK

Peter and the apostles replied, "We must obey God rather than people."—Acts 5:29

Abbey listened closely as Mrs. Williams told the Bible story about Peter and some of the other apostles who were put in prison just for preaching about Jesus. "I'm glad we don't live back in New Testament times. I can't believe they put people in prison just for talking about Jesus. It would be so scary if that was the law here. Would we obey the law or do what Peter did?!" Abbey exclaimed.

"We are blessed to be able to talk about Jesus in our country," Mrs. Williams said. "But there are many places in the world where people are still put in prison for telling others about Jesus. The Bible lets us know that we should honor authority, but when the laws go against God's laws, we have to make a choice. Many of our missionaries and other believers around the world are like Peter and choose to obey God rather than people."

NAIL IT DOWN

Have you heard the Bible story about Peter and the other apostles in prison? You can find the story and read about it in your Bible in Acts 5:12–32.

PRAY

Ask God to be with missionaries and other believers around the world who have to risk prison or worse when they choose to obey God.

90

IF AT ALL POSSIBLE

If possible, as far as it depends on you, live at peace with everyone.—Romans 12:18

Jesus told His followers that they were to love their neighbors (other people) as they loved themselves. When you treat people the way you want to be treated, you are obeying God, but what about the people who seem impossible to get along with? Even when you try to be kind, they say mean things or make jokes about you or even try to make you angry. Many of the commands we read in the Bible are pretty clear. Do this or don't do that, but this is one command that says "if possible," and "as far as it depends on you." In other words, do the best you can to be at peace or get along with others. God knows you are only responsible for your own actions. Sometimes, you can't help how others act, but you can obey God with your actions.

PERSONAL BLUEPRINT

Do you know some people who are difficult to get along with? Don't write names, but jot some initials here. Then pray for them.

PRAY

Praying for people who are unkind to you can help you feel better. And asking God to work in their hearts is a great thing to do too. Only God can truly change people.

91

GOD PROVIDES A WAY

But God is faithful; he will not allow you to be tempted beyond what you are able, but with the temptation he will also provide a way out so that you may be able to bear it.—1 Corinthians 10:13

Brett had gotten in trouble at school again. He talked with his dad on the car ride home. Dad reminded Brett what the Bible teaches about doing the right thing. Suddenly, Brett exclaimed, "I wish I lived back in Bible times. It must have been a whole lot easier to never get in trouble!"

"Sorry, Brett," Dad said, "Sin was still sin back then as it is today. We have lots of things they didn't have back then as far as technology or possessions, but greed, selfishness, anger, and other emotions and thoughts that lead us to sin are the same. God is the same today as He was then. He always provides a way for you to resist the temptation to do wrong, but you have to be willing to take the way out that God provides."

PERSONAL BLUEPRINT

God does not tempt us to do wrong. Instead, He provides ways we can resist temptation. Here are a few ways. Can you add a few more?

Walk away.

Pray.

Listen before responding.

Ask a friend for help.

PRAY

What are you most often tempted to do? Ask God to help you know the way of escape He is giving you and ask Him for the courage to take it.

92

PART OF THE PLAN

For we are his workmanship, created in Christ Jesus for good works, which God prepared ahead of time for us to do.—Ephesians 2:10

"We have to write about what we want to be when we grow up," Charlotte told her mom. "I don't know what to write. I'm not good at anything! I mostly just like to read books."

"You are exactly the person God made you to be," her mom replied. "God created you to do good things, and He has already prepared those things for you. When you were little you liked to set the table. You couldn't reach the dishes, so I put them on the table for you. I prepared them so you could do a good job. God has prepared things for you. Each day you follow Jesus, you are becoming the person God planned for you to be. Someday, you will see how God has been preparing you. Reading books may be part of that preparation since you like it so much. I'm excited to see what God has planned for you."

PERSONAL BLUEPRINT

Answer these questions about yourself. Someday, you may see how God was preparing you.

> What is your best class in school?
>
> What do you like to do when you are by yourself?
>
> What do people often compliment you about?
>
> What is something that is easy for you but harder for some other people you know?

PRAY

Thank God for the plans He has for you. Pray that He will help you obey Him so you are prepared for His special plans.

93

OBEYING PARENTS

Children, obey your parents in the Lord, because this is right.—Ephesians 6:1

Mr. Luke's class had just read Ephesians 6:1. Ian leaned back in his chair, "That's the verse parents always like to remember!" he exclaimed. "I'll be glad when I'm an adult and I don't have to do that commandment anymore."

Mr. Luke chuckled. "Sorry, Ian, but that commandment doesn't have an age limit. Being respectful to parents is something all ages should do. Paul was writing this letter to the church at Ephesus. He quoted several parts of Scripture in his letter. He even reminded the people that when God first gave this commandment as part of the Ten Commandments, it was the only one that came with a promise. If the people obeyed this commandment, God promised that it would go well with them in the promised land. Obeying parents is an important way to obey God."

NAIL IT DOWN

Paul quoted from what we call the Old Testament. See if you can find these verses in your Bible.

Exodus 20:12

Deuteronomy 5:16

PRAY

Parents aren't always right, but they are still your parents. Ask God to help you obey and respect your parents in the ways you should.

94

OBEDIENCE AND ATTITUDE

And whatever you do, in word or in deed,
do everything in the name of the Lord Jesus,
giving thanks to God the Father through him.
—Colossians 3:17

Rachel knew it was her turn to clean the rabbit cage. Rachel really hated that job. How could two cute bunnies like Poppy and Cobb create such a smelly mess? "I know!" Rachel thought. "I'll go read my Bible for a bit first." Deep down Rachel knew she was just avoiding the job, but surely reading her Bible was okay in order to avoid the dreaded chore. She looked up the verse listed in her devotional guide. It was Colossians 3:17. The words caught her by surprise. "Whatever you do . . . do everything in the name of the Lord Jesus, giving thanks to God." Everything? Even cleaning smelly rabbit cages? Rachel realized the cage had to be cleaned whether she wanted to or not. She could grumble the whole time, or she could do it and give thanks to God for Poppy and Cobb while she cleaned. Maybe a better attitude would make the job easier.

PERSONAL BLUEPRINT

Write about some things you have to do that you dread. Think about how you can do those things with a thankful heart instead. List your ideas.

PRAY

Everyone has to do things they don't prefer to do. Ask God to help you remember that you are doing things for Him and thank Him for the ability to do them.

95

OBEYING AUTHORITIES

Remind them to submit to rulers and authorities,
to obey, to be ready for every good work.
—Titus 3:1

"I'm tired of being bossed around," Eli muttered. "My teacher gives me assignments. My band director makes me practice. My coach says to run laps. I can't wait until I'm older and I'm my own boss!"

"You sound upset," Uncle Jeff said. He had just arrived to give Eli a ride home.

"I am!" Eli said. "People tell me what to do all the time."

Uncle Jeff laughed, "I hate to tell you this, but you will always have people in authority over you. If you have a job, it'll be your boss. If you drive, you have to obey the laws." Eli looked discouraged. "But that's not something to be discouraged about," Uncle Jeff continued. "The Bible tells us that we are to obey those authorities and be ready to do the best job we can. God is the ultimate authority. When we obey the people He has put over us, we are actually obeying Him."

NAIL IT DOWN

Sometimes the religious leaders tried to trick Jesus so they could accuse Him of breaking a law. You can read about one of those times in Luke 20:20–26. How did Jesus obey God and still respect authority?

PRAY

Instead of grumbling about people in authority over you, pray for them. Praying for your teachers, leaders, and parents is a blessing to them and to you.

96

CHEERFUL OBEDIENCE

*Don't neglect to do what is good and to share,
for God is pleased with such sacrifices.*
—Hebrews 13:16

Madi picked up the basket of toys she had chosen to give away. Madi had carefully picked toys that seemed new and still fun to play with. She brought her toy basket to the kitchen. Her mom had also gathered things for the toys and clothing collection. "Madi, I'm so proud of you," Mom said. "Do you know what a sacrifice is?" Madi looked puzzled. "A sacrifice means giving up something precious as an offering to God. I can tell you chose toys that you still enjoy."

"We talked about the toy and clothing collection at church on Sunday," Madi said. "Our teacher explained *why* we give is even more important than *what* we give. If we give as if we are giving to God, then it is a true offering. I didn't just want to give what I didn't want anymore. I wanted to give my toys to please God."

"Wow!" Mom exclaimed. "Your teacher explained it well."

PERSONAL BLUEPRINT

Think of something you can share or something you can do because you want to please God. Draw a picture of it here.

PRAY

Ask God to help you think of things you can share with others or do for others.

97

LOVING OBEDIENCE

For this is what love for God is: to keep his commands. And his commands are not a burden.—1 John 5:3

Some people think they have to live just right for God to love them. They think that if they mess up even a little, God won't accept them, but we know God loves us because He chooses to, not because of what we do. The Bible does have certain commands or rules. We are to love God with all our heart, soul, mind, and strength. We are to love others and treat them the way we want to be treated. We are to tell others about Jesus. When you think about it, God's rules are pretty basic. They aren't a burden. When you think about the things God has done for you, you know He loves you. As you realize how much you love God, then obeying His commands becomes what you want to do. There is nothing to fear. Love God and keep His commands because you love Him, not to earn His love. He already loves you more than you can imagine.

NAIL IT DOWN

John was one of Jesus' original twelve disciples. He wrote five New Testament books: John, 1 John, 2 John, 3 John, and Revelation. John wrote a lot about God's love for us and the love we should have for God. You may have memorized one of the verses John wrote about God's love. Can you quote John 3:16 from memory? If not, look it up and mark it in your Bible

PRAY

Thank God for His amazing love for you. Tell God about your love for Him.

WALKING IN TRUTH

I have no greater joy than this: to hear that my children are walking in truth.—3 John 1:4

You may not realize this, but a lot of people are part of helping you grow to know about God. Think about people in your family, in your church, or friends who have helped you know more about the Bible, about God, and His Son Jesus. One of the greatest joys for Christian adults is to see or hear about kids they have taught who are choosing to follow God. In today's verse, John said he had "no greater joy" than to hear that his children were walking in the truth. His children were all the people who had listened to His teaching about Jesus. "Walking in truth," means that a person lives in ways that honor and please God. When you honor God, you are also bringing joy to those who know you and also follow Jesus.

PERSONAL BLUEPRINT

Think about the people who have helped you know about God, Jesus, and the Bible. Write their names here.

PRAY

Thank God for all the people on your list. Thank God that someday you will be the one who will help someone know about Him.

99

A FIRM FOUNDATION

Therefore, everyone who hears these words of mine and acts on them will be like a wise man who built his house on the rock.—Matthew 7:24

The Sermon on the Mount is the longest section of Jesus' teachings in the Bible. It begins in Matthew chapter 5 and goes through chapter 7. As Jesus finished speaking, He told a parable. (*Parables* are stories Jesus told to help people understand the kingdom of God.) Jesus talked about two builders. One built his house on a foundation of sand. The other built his house on a foundation of rock. When storms came, the house on the sandy foundation collapsed as the sand was washed away, but the house on the rock was secure. Jesus said that everyone who listens to what He teaches will be like the wise builder. Our trust in Jesus gives us a strong foundation. Troubles will still come, but we know Jesus is with us and God is in control.

NAIL IT DOWN

Read the whole parable of the builders. You can find it in your Bible in Matthew 7:24–29.

For a bigger challenge, read the entire Sermon on the Mount (Matthew 5:1–7:29).

PRAY

Today may be a good day or a not-so-good day. Either way, God loves you and is with you. Thank God for the ways He cares for you.

100

KEEP BUILDING

But as for you, continue in what you have learned and firmly believed. You know those who taught you.—2 Timothy 3:14

Jack opened up the new notebook his Bible study teacher had given him. She suggested he use it to list people to pray for and to record Bible verses he wanted to remember. Jack had recently trusted Jesus as Savior. He was excited every time he learned something from the Bible. Jack decided to list the people who were helping him learn about God. He wanted to thank God for them and pray for them. Jack was surprised as the list grew longer. God had put a lot of people in his life to help him know about Jesus. Jack thought, *I hope I can tell someone one day what I know about God. I want people to know about Jesus just like all of these people wanted me to know about Him.*

PERSONAL BLUEPRINT

Wow! You've finished this book. Keep going. How will you continue your daily time with God? You can reread this book or find a new one. You can choose a chapter in the Bible and read it. Write about what you plan to do to continue your daily time with God.

PRAY

Thank God for all the things you've learned from the Bible. Ask God to help you want to keep reading His Word and telling others about Him.